Diana Peck

Christian Focus Publications

ISBN 1-85792-134-8

Published by
Christian Focus Publications Ltd
Geanies House, Fearn, Ross-shire,
IV20 1TW, Scotland, Great Britain.

Cover design by Donna Macleod

Printed and bound in Great Britain by
Cox & Wyman Ltd, Reading, Berkshire

Contents

1. I WAS DIFFERENT 4

2. A WAY OF LIFE 14

3. IN THE TRUTH 26

4. INSIDE A KINGDOM HALL 39

5. INSIDE A CHURCH 48

6. STILL DIFFERENT 57

7. AWAY FROM HOME 67

8. GOODBYE TO JEHOVAH GOD 82

9. THEY ARE DIFFERENT 88

10. SOMETHING IS MISSING 96

11. MARRIAGE IS WHAT I NEED 102

12. A DISTURBING ENCOUNTER 113

13. SOUND OF A CRY 120

14. WE ARE DIFFERENT 131

15. RETHINKING ALL I EVER KNEW 142

16. POSTSCRIPT 152

1

I WAS DIFFERENT

I couldn't reach the knocker, so Dad did it for me and walked away. A dog barked and I felt afraid. Perhaps there was no one in. I gazed at the shut door hopefully. But I had wanted to do this on my own. It was the summer of 1940, and I was eight years old, with a lot of experience behind me of knocking on doors - with someone else. Suddenly the door opened and I looked up at a tall lady staring into space with a puzzled expression.

'Good morning, would you please read my card?'

'Oh, there you are!' She looked down with a laugh. 'How on earth did you reach the knocker?'

She took the postcard size printed card in its cellophane wallet, glancing at it curiously. The heading was 'Testimony Card'. It was an explanation, a formal introduction, as to why I had come: 'We are Bible students calling at homes in your area to bring you a message of hope and comfort in today's troubled world. No doubt you feel concerned at what the future holds. We believe the Bible shows why the world is in such confusion and it will answer your questions.'

'How much are they?' the lady smiled, indicating

the magazines and books in my hand.

'Well, we don't really sell our literature, but we would be happy to leave one with you for a small donation to the Watchtower Society.'

She shouted back into the house, 'Shirley, dear, bring me my purse, I want to give this little girl some money.'

Shirley was about my own age. We smiled at one another weakly while her Mum selected a copy of *The Watchtower* magazine.

My Dad, who was hovering by the gate, moved in quickly to follow up on this apparent sign of interest. 'Good morning, Madam,' he said, touching his trilby hat with old-fashioned courtesy. 'I'm glad to see you're interested in our literature. We are living in very troubled times. The only hope for mankind is in Jehovah God and his purposes which the Bible reveals to us.'

Shirley's Mum nodded. 'Yes, there is a lot of trouble in this world everywhere. You wonder what's going to happen next.'

'Yes, Madam, the Bible teaches that these things are signs of the end times. Jehovah God is going to destroy this world's system and all its wickedness, and establish his kingdom of righteousness on earth. Could we come back, perhaps one evening when your husband is at home, and tell you more about these things?'

'I believe in God!' said the lady emphatically,

ignoring the question. 'And I go to church when I can, but it's not easy on Sundays because it's the only day my husband gets off.' Her tone appealed for sympathy.

But we were not there for that. We had a message to deliver and the aim to follow up any interested contact with a home Bible study.

'Which church is that?' enquired Dad.

On her answer would depend a whole string of ready-made conclusions. I knew that was why he asked. I'd followed this technique before.

'Oh, I'm Church of England, it's just down the road there.' She waved her hand vaguely in its direction.

I saw Dad's wry smile but he kept his views on the C of E to himself at this point. And I wondered how such a pleasant and friendly lady could possibly be one of those religious hypocrites who, I was told, inhabited the gloomy-looking places called churches. However, we were on the Lord's work and Dad repeated that all-important question, 'Could we call back one evening, then?'

'Well, yes, I suppose so, when would it be?'

'Whatever evening and time suit you best, Mrs er....?'

'Mayes.'

'Well, Mrs Mayes, we can come any time.'

That was true enough. The 'Lord's work' is priority for every Jehovah's Witness. The rest of life, if there is any, has to fit round that. Each is a whole-hearted, dedicated, servant of Jehovah, each must be a Witness.

'What about next Friday, about eight o'clock, then?'

'Will shc come as well?' This was Shirley speaking. But I shook my head.

Mrs Mayes watched Dad write the details of the back-call on a slip of paper in his hand. Then Dad touched his trilby again, told her his name was Mr Mitchell, gave her a couple of back numbers of *Awake* magazine for free, and off we went.

I felt like a dog with two tails, after all I was the one who first knocked at the door, well tried to anyway. But certainly I had presented the testimony card and started things going.

The testimony card was one way in which we approached people on the doors. It was usually used by the less eloquent, or more nervous beginners. Experienced Witnesses speak directly and frequently non-stop to the person who opens their door.

Another method we used, which delighted me, was a small portable phonograph (American term for gramophone), with a recorded talk from the president of the Watchtower Society. I always enjoyed winding it up and seeing how other occupants of the house would emerge to listen out of curiosity.

Every call we made was recorded on Report Slips with details of literature placed, interest shown and of course the date arranged for a return call or follow-up to the initial contact. These would be kept on file at the Kingdom Hall for future reference for anyone else later working those same streets.

Mostly, I recall people reacted pleasantly to us. But there was one occasion indelibly printed on my mind.

'Take your b........ books and get the hell out of here!' The voice was shrill and I turned to see a woman angrily pursuing two Jehovah's Witnesses down her garden path, arms waving.

The shrieking continued, 'If I had my way, I'd put the lot of you up against a wall and shoot you. You won't fight in the war, will you? My son did and he's been killed. B....... conscientious objectors. Don't you dare knock at my door again.'

Sweeping up to one of the Witnesses, an elderly lady, she brought her raised hand down on her arm, knocking the books she carried from her and kicking them round the pavement.

My Dad was in charge of the assignment, and he called to the other Witnesses in the street and insisted we moved away quickly. By now the shrieks had brought the neighbours out of their doors and they stood watching silently, one or two seemed amused. Feeling frightened I walked quickly with the others, round the corner out of sight and there we grouped together and conferred.

This was the first time I'd seen something like

this happen and I wanted to go home, away from the ugly scene. She'd said she'd like to shoot us all! What if she had a gun? Fearfully I stood listening to the adults' conversation. They didn't sound at all afraid. 'Persecuted for righteousness sake,' my Dad was saying authoritatively.

He was short in stature and slight, but his voice was unfalteringly strong and confident as he reassured us such things were only to be expected from enemies of the Truth. 'We shan't turn tail and run, we'll move on to the next street.'

I groaned inwardly, but dared not admit I was frightened. Before long everyone seemed regaled and impassioned with zeal for righteousness and, savouring an air of martyrdom, we walked on to the next street to continue door-knocking.

I do not recall any love or concern being expressed for the angry woman. It was 'To the work, to the work, Oh ye servants of God, let us follow the path that the Master hath trod'. This was a favourite hymn I enjoyed singing at the Kingdom Hall. Out in the violent street I wasn't so keen.

'Conscientious objectors.' I knew that term very well for I was aware that many Jehovah's Witnesses went to prison during the war rather than join the armed services.

Often the full-time workers, or pioneers as they were called, came to our home for a meal. Dad, as leader of a Kingdom Hall, had spoken for many of them at the tribunals for conscientious objectors. Some were permitted to do farm work but many went to prison. I also knew that members of the Jehovah's Witnesses' organisation in Germany did not get the option. They were shot if they refused to fight.

These things were talked about around our meal table, together with such Biblical references as 'Jesus said, "My kingdom is not of this world. If my kingdom were of this world, then would my servants fight".'

'Hold your Union Jack up high when we stand to sing the national anthem.' The teacher beamed brightly at the group of children in front of her.

I was one of them. And although my understanding of all the issues involved was limited, I knew for sure this was one thing my Dad would not like me to do.

I trembled inwardly at the thought of what he would say if he could see me taking part in this idol worship. I knew that was what he would call it. I'd heard him say so often on our door-to-door visiting. Saluting any flag, singing the national anthem, were quite wrong for anyone who served Jehovah God.

But with a sense of guilt I joined in with the others. I didn't really know what to say, and more than anything I was afraid of being marked out as different. So I waved the Union Jack and feebly mouthed 'God save our gracious king', hoping fervently that the wrath of Jehovah God would not fall on me. And, more to the point, my parents would not get to know of my brief period of idol worship.

'All in together, girls, never mind the weather, girls. Come on in, Diana!' shouted Vera, as the long skipping rope was turned.

It was playtime and, as usual, Vera Parker had got everybody organised. She was a bit of a bossy boots and it didn't auger well for any classmate to dispute with her, so in I jumped.

'My Auntie's baby is being christened in the church on Sunday, and afterwards we've got a big family party,' Vera's long fair hair blew in the wind as we bobbed up and down.

Suddenly I felt irritated. Vera had been on about her Auntie's baby for weeks. I was fed up hearing about it.

'Christening's nothing. It doesn't do anything for you.'

'What d'you mean? Everyone gets christened. That's how you get your name.'

'Well, we don't believe in it. I haven't been christened.'

'Well, then, you haven't got a proper name.'

The rope stopped suddenly as Vera caught her foot in it.

'Did you hear that?' she demanded of the other

skippers. 'She's never been christened. So she hasn't got a proper name. We can call her anything we like.'

She giggled and started trotting out a spiel of names, trying to decide which one to settle for. Mercifully, the bell rang, playtime was over. I still felt irritated with Vera, and miserable now as well.

I told my mother when I got home. 'I don't think Vera wants to be my friend any more,' I moaned.

Mum was not too fond of Vera as my friend anyway, mainly because she dominated me, or tried to, and her Mum smoked, wore bright lipstick and was 'always gossiping to someone or other up at the Co-op at the end of our road.

'Don't take any notice,' she said brusquely. 'You tell her, sticks and stones may break my bones but names will never hurt me.'

I suppose it was a good enough answer, but I doubted if it would shut Vera up. Anyway it did hurt, the names she mockingly called me. But her campaign didn't last long.

There is no ceremony or act of dedication for a baby in Jehovah's Witnesses. Children are 'covered' by their parents until they reach an age of understanding when they can be baptised by full immersion in water. The Witnesses regard this as the Biblical pattern and put the responsibility on the parents to see their children are brought up in 'the fear and admonition of the Lord'. Christening is ridiculed as a nonsense act, as yet another example of the duplicity of religious rigmarole. So what if I was different from everyone else at school. If they were taught to believe that something like christening was necessary, then I was sorry they were so wrong.

'Do you know why Mr Jones is so anxious for all children to be vaccinated?' It was my class teacher talking to me.

I shook my head. How should I know about the headmaster's anxieties?

'Several years ago,' she continued, 'Mr Jones' little boy died of diphtheria. He says it was so quick, like a candle blown out. You tell your parents that, will you?'

I nodded but knew it wouldn't make any difference. But the teacher's words made me feel unhappy, insecure. Could I die if I wasn't vaccinated?

When I dutifully relayed the teacher's message, Dad reassured me that we lived under the protection of Jehovah God. Then he picked up his pen and wrote a letter to the headmaster explaining his Bible-based reasons for refusing permission for vaccination.

My anxieties were quelled as I sensed his unwavering, undisturbed attitude. With his confidence in Jehovah God, everything must be all right and I wouldn't die.

2

A WAY OF LIFE

Our large terraced house in Abbey Wood, South-East London, stood solidly between the houses of the Prentice and the Cramp families.

Mrs Prentice, I learned, was demon-possessed. This was not something gleaned from my favourite occupation of eavesdropping on adult conversations. But it was Dad's quite matter-of-fact explanation for all the rows and rumpus, the screeching and swearing, that floated regularly over the garden fence from next door. Sounds that even penetrated our house if windows and doors were not tightly shut.

I could accept his explanation without question. I'd heard such things mentioned amongst the Witnesses on our doorstep calls. I felt sorry for Stanley, her 'little devil', as she called her son, who was usually the target for her hysterical shrieks, threats and thrashings.

But behind the higher part of the fence separating the concrete of our backyards, I practised my skipping without any fear of the woman next door. I knew we were quite safe in the Watchtower from any evil power.

One Saturday morning, as I pushed Vera on the garden swing, a loud wailing and shouting suddenly pierced the air.

'You little devil, I'll give you what for, you see if I don't!' Red-faced, brawny arms waving wildly, Mrs Prentice charged down the garden after the howling Stanley. As her voice rose in a crescendo of expletives, Vera jumped off the swing and faced me questioningly. I decided to tell her straight.

'She's demon-possessed, she's always going off like that, she lives down the pub, smokes like a chimney and uses filthy language all the time.' Parrot-like, and with an air of authority, I repeated the phrases I'd heard.

But Vera was not impressed with my definitive judgment. After all, her Mum smoked, drank Guinness and had hysterics sometimes, though in a more refined way. She shook her head and narrowed her eyes in disagreement. 'It's because of her nerves. That's what the doctor tells my Mum. She takes tablets for it, and drinks Guinness for a tonic. The doctor told her to.'

Of course, I knew Vera wouldn't believe me. I lived in a different world to her most of the time. But I knew too that I wouldn't have swopped places with her for anything. There were no hysterics in my home, no shouted tirades or tantrums. A calm contentment filled the air.

We lived with Mum's parents - Grandfather and

Nan - but had our separate living rooms. They were not in Jehovah's Witnesses. The centres of their lives were the off-licence at the corner of our road and the allotment a bit further on.

I enjoyed both when given the chance. Nan would send me to the off-licence with some money for lemonade and crisps and a sealed envelope in a shopping bag which I handed over to Mr Taylor. In exchange he would put two brown bottles in the bag.

Nan made a great fuss of me for doing this little errand for her, but always asked me not to mention it to anyone. I kept the secret until, one dreadful day, Nan's alcoholism was exposed, and my innocent trips to the off-licence came to an abrupt end.

Next to the Prentice's lived a tall, disdainful-looking woman with a short, timid-looking husband. They were the Waters who kept themselves aloof, barely bothering to nod acknowledgement to anyone they passed in the street. 'Toffee-nosed,' Nan would say with a sniff, as she peered from behind the net curtains in her front room.

Then a strange thing happened. I overheard Mum telling Nan, 'You know that Mrs Waters down the road? Well, something awful has happened to her.'

I hovered in the passageway by Nan's half-open kitchen door, ears wide open.

'Hasn't she been in hospital? I haven't seen her walk up the road for some time.'

'Yes, but she's come home and her mouth has

gone horribly crooked and her jaw shakes so much she can hardly eat.'

'Good lor',' muttered Nan. 'Have you seen her?'

'Not properly. Next door told me up at the Co-op, and when I came home she was hurrying up the road on the opposite side, with Mr Waters. She had a big scarf wrapped round half her face.'

When the story was retold to Dad at teatime, I mustered an expression of innocence and felt slightly chagrined about my eavesdropping in the passage. Obviously I needn't have bothered.

But Dad's response gripped me.

'It's strange, isn't it?' he said slowly. 'Some weeks ago she was very slanderous to old Wrighty on the doorstep. Don't you remember, he came in and told us how she'd let off at him and the Watchtower Society something dreadful. She called him all the names under the sun and said some vicious things about Jehovah's Witnesses. She told him never to call at her house again.

'Old Wrighty was very upset about it. And he's such a mild-mannered man too. Sounds like this mouth affliction might be a judgment on her. The Almighty deals with those who oppose his people.'

Mum, as usual, quietly acquiesced with Dad's comments. I sat silent, revelling in the strong sense of security and specialness that was my heritage. At times like this I didn't mind about feeling different. I was happy that we were in the Jehovah's Witnesses and following a way of life in the service of Jehovah God.

Everyone in our street was having an air-raid shelter dug-out in their garden. Everyone except us it seemed.

'We don't need one of those!' Dad was adamant.

'We shan't have any garden left with one of them things,' muttered Grandfather.

That was before the blitz began. Once the air-raid sirens started up regularly every night, and the bombs began to fall, Mum, me, and my sister slept under the table on a mattress. Dad fixed himself up with a palliasse in the cupboard under the stairs. Grandfather and Nan took up the invitation of the elderly Mr and Mrs Tubb, next door to the Cramps, to share their dug-out.

But after a couple of weeks of this nightly arrangement the novelty palled. And there were other factors.

'I think we really ought to have our own shelter if these raids are going on. We don't want to depend on the neighbours,' Mum appealed to Dad who looked faintly surprised. He certainly wasn't depending on the neighbours and didn't think she was either.

Then she explained: 'Diana and me went in Tubb's dug-out with Nan yesterday afternoon. Poor Mr Tubb is very ill, and in a lot of pain. He was just lying on the bunk groaning and saying, "Stick a knife in me". It wasn't very nice for Diana sitting there, I felt sorry for her.'

From my eavesdropping niche in the passage, I nodded and felt sorry for myself. I wanted to barge in and back Mum up because I certainly didn't want to go to Tubb's shelter again. But would Dad understand?

Then Mum delivered the coup de grâce: 'And now Mrs Prentice has said that Diana can go in their shelter any time. I don't like that idea either.'

'No, certainly not. She mustn't go in there!' Dad's firm voice was so reassuring. 'I'll go and talk to Grandfather about it.'

Swiftly I bolted up the stairs before Dad emerged from the living room and walked briskly down the passage to Nan's kitchen.

Within days our rectangle of earth was churned up. Sand, cement, and bricks were being carried through the house, a concrete slab laid down and our shelter erected. Not a dug-out, like the neighbours. No doubt, supplies had run out by the time we were precipitated into having one. Ours was a seven-foot high brick shelter which left space in the garden only for the swing, a meagre border of plants and a peony bush.

'I shan't go in it!' Dad stoutly informed us. 'I'm alright under the stairs.'

Mum looked upset and I felt worried, but Grandfather gave one of his hearty chuckles. 'That's right, you've got someone looking after you. Us miserable sinners need a shelter.'

Dad didn't argue with him, he never did. And when Nan murmured anxiously, 'I hope you'll be all right and they don't drop a bomb on the house,' he simply said quietly, 'I shall be all right, don't you worry. The house will be all right too. The Almighty will protect us.'

His faith was like a warm blanket to me, and secretly I wished I could stay with him in the cupboard under the stairs. It seemed the safest place on earth just then. How deeply I admired his courage and unwavering faith.

But Mum soon applied her homemaking skills and turned the brick shelter into a homely place with rag rugs, cosy cushions and bunk beds, and we slept there every night.

'Vera's going to join the Brownies. Why don't you join as well?'

It was Vera's Mum speaking. I felt the usual lump of lead lodge itself inside me. How could I explain to Mrs Parker that I couldn't possibly join?

I'd already tried to explain to Vera, when I told her about Armageddon and judgment and how all the vicars and churches had got everything wrong, they were all evil servants. Especially as they go around blessing guns and drums and battleships. 'And Brownies are all part of this world's system,'

I told her, blithely relaying phrases gleaned from the adult company I kept.

Trying to tell Vera's Mum the same things was not so easy. I guessed Vera had asked her Mum to persuade me, and I was always a bit afraid of upsetting Mrs Parker and sending her off into hysterics.

'No, I can't join the Brownies. It's a church organisation, and my Mum and Dad don't agree with wearing a uniform. You have to salute the flag and that sort of thing ...'.

Lamely words petered out as I saw the storm brewing in her face. She was going to go off the deep end at me. Oh help! But her grim expression puckered suddenly into laughter.

'Don't be daft! There's nothing wrong with Brownies. Be nice for my Vera to have a friend to go with. You ask your Mum if she'll let you go, there's a good girl.'

She lit a cigarette and laughed again.

I felt very uncomfortable, I'd have preferred hysterics to being laughed at.

Vera looked sharply at me. She didn't have to speak, she was saying with that look, 'Are you going to do what I want you to do or be standoffish and stupid?'

But there was no doubt in my mind. I would never go to Brownies or anything else connected with that place called church.

Being Vera's friend caused a few problems. She was so confident about everything, and her parents let her do anything. She led and I followed.

We were avid readers of *Anne of Green Gables* in our junior years, and Vera saw herself as Anne, whose best friend was called Diana. That's why she insisted I was her best friend. There was a compulsion about her, although in many situations with her I felt decidedly uneasy. Like the summer's evening she wanted to try out her new roller skates.

Skates and a bicycle were two things I was not permitted to have. That was nothing to do with being in the Jehovah's Witnesses, but an over-protective attitude of my parents. So, I was all for helping Vera try her skates.

'Let's start down your road, it's got a good slope,' she grinned cheerfully, and my heart sank.

'No, not until my Dad's gone out. He'll be going out about seven. Let's go in the next road along first.'

'All right then, if you like.'

Thankfully, for once Vera was willing to do things my way. I hoped she would be happy to stay in the next road because, even if Dad was out doing his return-calls, there was the other problem of Nan seated behind the net curtains.

How thrilling it all was! With one skate each, we held hands and sailed down the street once, twice, and then times without number. It was worth the breathless walk back up the hill just to skate down again and again. It was intoxicating.

'I want to do this forever and forever, don't you, Diana?'

I nodded happily, and then conscience struck. 'But I think I'd better go home now, Vera. It must be getting late, we've been here for ages.'

'Well, let's go and have a last skate down your road. Your Dad must have gone out by now.'

'Yes ... but ... oh, blow it! Let's go.'

Blow everything, I thought, it's all too good to stop now.

Once down the road past our house and the intrepid Vera started running back up the hill shouting, 'Once more, come on, this is the last time.'

I obeyed unhesitatingly, the thrill of one foot on a roller skate had me hooked. Hand-in-hand, we careered down again and collapsed in laughter. Helping each other up, we began walking back when I froze to a standstill.

'It's my Dad!' I gasped.

The familiar figure, briefcase in hand, was waiting at the gate.

'Come on,' urged Vera, 'you can't just stand here.'

I walked slowly towards him, feeling terror-struck at what he would say. He never hit me, never hurt me, but I hated to displease him, and surely I had done just that. I smiled weakly at him as I drew near.

With astonishment I realised he was smiling too.

'You must come in now and have your glory washed.'

'What?' I floundered, wondering what sort of code this was for a telling-off.

'The Bible says a woman's hair is her glory and your mother is waiting to wash yours.'

And with that he turned and walked up the road.

I stood there feeling relieved, amazed and a bit stupid all at once. I was aware of Vera standing there also, arms folded, and a defiant look. Just let him tell her off for lending me a roller skate and there'd be a sharp retort roll off her tongue. Vera simply wasn't afraid of anyone, no not even Jehovah God. If only I didn't have to live up to being her best friend just because of my name.

'Your name is in the Bible, I found it the other day.'

I stared at Douglas unbelievingly. He was a few years older than me and a bit superior with his knowledge. But how come he knew something I didn't about my name?

'I was sure it must be in there. I mean what with your Dad in charge of the Kingdom Hall and being such a Bible student, you'd think it was quite likely, wouldn't you?'

But it was news to me. I had never been told so.

Douglas opened his Bible and pointed out the words: 'Great is Diana of the Ephesians'. I was very impressed and didn't bother to read on. Just as well perhaps. I would have felt confused then to discover it was the name of a heathen goddess, an idol.

I wondered whether I should tell Vera about my name, but decided against it. She might get upset about her Anne of Green Gables best friend having other connections!

3

IN THE TRUTH

One day I dared to defy Vera.

She insisted we should go exploring in the woods next to the recreation ground. 'No, I can't!' I protested, stopping abruptly at the entrance gate. All Mum's warnings about playing in the woods surged against Vera's suggestion. As much as I feared upsetting Vera, I feared more what might happen to me if I didn't heed those warnings.

Impatiently Vera opened the gate and stalked confidently along the narrow path. She didn't even look back, she assumed I would follow.

'I'm not coming, Vera, so there!' I shouted, then turned and fled.

'Diana! come back!'

I heard the command of shrill insistence, but I was in flight away from her, and courage rose as I ran. I could not, would not turn back. Propelled by the spur of conscience, I ran until I put the distance of sight and sound between us. Only then I slowed down, thankful Vera had not pursued me.

But for the first time ever, I had defied her. I reckoned there would be a price to pay - sharp words from Vera's tongue. She would find me again soon, and I needed to prepare for her fury. So instead of turning left for home, I turned right towards the railway crossing and the allotments.

If God's kingdom was to be established on earth 'as it is in heaven', which I was taught was to happen soon, I always imagined it would be something like Grandfather's plot, for it was a world of delight to me.

There were blackcurrants, strawberries, gooseberries, runner beans and peas to pick in season, or I could tend my own small patch of earth, beside the hut, where Grandfather helped me to grow clusters of bright nasturtiums, the lovely yellow mignonette and sweet-scented stock.

There were frogs and green slime in the well, birds nesting in the trees, the haunting call of wood pigeons, and the sound of the occasional train chuffing along all helped to make this an enchanted place for me.

Even in wintertime it was an excitement to help break the ice on the well and throw in the bucket on a rope.

And there was always the compost heap. This mound of organic manure was surrounded by large slabs of concrete and provided one of my favourite pastimes. It was a challenge to see if I could walk all round on the slabs without falling off.

'Hello duck! Come to pick the fruit?' If Grandfather sensed I was frightened and unhappy that summer evening I ran from Vera he never probed. It was a balm to my sore loneliness just to be welcomed as usual and be given something to do.

As I picked the strawberries, and ate most of them, confidence returned and I felt ready for the challenge of the compost heap. So there I was, with arms outstretched, wobbling precariously, practising my balancing act, when I saw a small fair-haired determined figure marching purposefully towards me.

'I've been looking everywhere for you!' she exploded. 'I've been all round the rec and the park and called at your house. Why did you run off like that? You might have said you were going to the plot. I don't think much of you for a friend ...'.

The words stung, but maintaining my superior position on the slabs of the compost heap I was able to look down at Vera without shame or remorse. I knew I'd done the right thing, the thing that would please my mother.

Grandfather came across and, as Vera complained bitterly to him about my behaviour, he suggested I should go home and put my mother's mind at rest. Although she had told Vera I was probably on the allotment she didn't know for sure. So reluctantly I left with the infuriated Vera, and we walked home in silence. As I parted from her to go indoors, she delivered a further sharp tirade.

The front door opened as I approached - Mum

had been watching the confrontation from the window. Thankfully, I tumbled indoors, crying.

'I told Vera you'd be on Grandad's plot. She's annoyed with you, isn't she?'

Tearfully I told Mum what had happened.

'I'm glad you did the right thing,' she said as she hugged me.

'You're the best friend I've got,' I murmured into her pinafore.

What a haven there was in this place called home!

There was a cooling-off period with Vera after this incident. I had broken her domination and things would never be quite the same again. I knew she had other friends who went happily to Brownies with her, and I began to see a lot more of another schoolfriend, Gwennie.

We walked home from school together, and from my house Gwennie walked on towards the allotments and her house in The Grove.

This was an area looked down upon by some who lived in more prestigious surroundings. Several of the terraced houses were squat and shabby, and the people who lived in them were spoken of disparagingly. Vera for one made it plain she despised my association with Gwennie.

But my mother liked my quiet, softly spoken, brown-haired little friend and was pleased I was spending more time with her. Our Jehovah's Witness friend, Old Wrighty, who had first knocked on

Dad's door with the Watchtower message, also lived in The Grove. Although his wife and family were very opposed to him for being a JW, and very nasty to him, as I learned one eavesdropping session, he was esteemed highly by everyone in my house for his firm stand for the Truth.

Gwennie's Mum was very placid like my mother, but I thought she always looked worried and tired. Their house seemed very poky for Gwennie and her two grown-up brothers and sister, with worn lino and frayed chair covers. I knew they must be very poor, but when Old Wrighty knocked on their door with the kingdom message they would listen gladly.

Gwennie would come down to the allotment with me, and always Grandfather would give her something, a cabbage perhaps, to take home.

I could never understand why Gwennie's mother got so excited about a cabbage. But her face would light up with pleasure and her thankyous were almost overwhelming. I didn't care for cabbage, but had to eat it of course. And I never knew a time when there was no food in my house, or ever sensed my mother was worried about making ends meet.

Money was certainly not plentiful, but I knew Mum kept meticulous accounts. Every Friday evening I watched fascinated as she sat at the oil-cloth-covered table in our living room and counted out Dad's wage packet. On a large sheet of paper she would enter figures and put money into small envelopes, stored in a large black wallet with a thick rubber band round it to hold them all together.

I always had plenty of questions about this activity, but invariably she would say, 'Don't interrupt me, I'm counting.' She did, however, impress upon me her great fear of getting into debt. 'I'd rather go without than buy something we can't afford. Out of debt, out of danger,' she nodded at me across the table.

So every week she put the money into separate envelopes to pay the bills and kept a written record. I would study the headed columns on her budget sheet, but her hieroglyphics were unfathomable and the figures fuddled me.

The attitude to money amongst committed Jehovah's Witnesses is the Biblical viewpoint of material values taking second place to spiritual values, as they study to have the knowledge of God's purposes. 'Owe no man anything' and giving a tithe to the 'Lord's work' as well as freewill offerings are consistent practices. Of course the sale of literature brings revenue into the Society, but members do contribute generously. And financial support for full-time workers, pioneers as we called them, would come mainly from those at their Kingdom Hall, with only a small allowance from the Watchtower Society.

One evening a week I usually went, with my parents, to Auntie Amy's house, just round the corner in the main road, where we met for a home Bible study. Although called a Bible study this was really a study of the latest Watchtower book.

In earlier years I would pass the time, in her comfortable sitting-room, with crayons and colouring books or something to make. Auntie Amy, being an infants' teacher, understood my needs. But at the age of nine, I was encouraged to take part in the study by reading aloud. I loved doing this because I could read well for my age, and people always commented on that fact.

The procedure was to read aloud a paragraph from the Watchtower book, and then answer the questions on it which were printed at the bottom of the page. The answer had to come, virtually word for word, from what had just been read. Then we'd look up the Bible reference which backed up the answer from the paragraph.

This simple question and answer method of 'study' is tantamount to brainwashing or indoctrination, but it is a very effective learning process, as has been proved in other organisations besides Jehovah's Witnesses. Not that I realised this at the time, of course. The ability to acquire knowledge in such an effortless way is attractive to many. It partly contributes to the Witnesses' feeling of superiority when they come to your door, Bible in hand.

Anyway, whatever was happening through this system of study, the enjoyable thing for me was the reading aloud. It made me feel important, and I prided myself on getting it right.

Not that I didn't have a few problems with the Authorized Version which was always used before the Watchtower published their own version, *The New World Translation of the Bible*. Reading once about Solomon, I said, 'He had many wives and cucumbers!' My Mother's smothered mirth made me pause.

'Wives and concubines,' corrected Dad patiently.

'What are they?' I wanted to know.

I cannot remember being given a satisfactory explanation, but I did understand they had no connection whatsoever with cucumbers. And I thought it had been a good guess on my part!

'Who is on the Lord's side, who will serve the King.
Who will be his witness, kingdom tidings bring.'

The vast congregation would rise as one to sing the stirring hymn. It was the time of a great convention, a very important event for all Jehovah's Witnesses, bringing together thousands of adherents from all over the world. Leaders of the movement, from the American-based hierarchy are there to address the faithful. Hundreds will often be baptised by immersion in the local swimming pool.

I asked to be baptised when I was nine years old. I had no idea what it meant, my only reason was that I knew it would please my Dad. I'd realised by then that life was a lot smoother if one pleased one's parents. So, donning a swimsuit, I stepped into the pool surrounded by people who clapped and cheered. How good I felt!

At convention time a new publication is usually launched, which will be studied in the home Bible study and also offered to interested people Witnesses meet on the doorstep.

And for sure, the main thrust of the meetings would be the signs of the times, the time is short and Armageddon is near.

I might have wriggled a bit with boredom as a speaker went on, but the sense of urgency and specialness of the people gathered there made a deep impression on me. We were God's people, no one else could be because we only had the 'Truth'.

Truth was an important word I knew. Especially when one of our Witness friends made up a poem and wrote it in my autograph book:

Joan and Alice and Ruth and Nell
Went one day to the wishing well.
Each at wishing played her part
With a wish wished deep in an eager heart.

'I wish for sparkling jewels,' cried Nell.
'Yes, diamonds and rubies,' said Joan as well.
'Give me dresses,' said flighty Alice,
'A beautiful home, a stately palace.'

'And what do you wish for? Tell us, Ruth.'
Her wish was best of all, t'was 'Truth'.

Yes, a very important word and we were *in* 'The Truth', you couldn't get more important than that. Nothing, nobody, was right outside of us.

So a great sense of self-worth, of purpose, was in everyone and it was constantly reinforced by the talks given at conventions. Any exposition of Scripture was related at every point to 'God's little flock who would receive the kingdom'. That was us. A little group of believers pitted against this world's might as well as every religious system.

It was like being in another world at these conventions. Buildings and grounds of places such as the De Montfort Hall in Leicester were taken over for a week. All attending were found bed and breakfast accommodation in the homes of local people. Huge marquees were erected in the grounds where meals were served, and literature, records and information displayed. It was a monument of organisational skill on the part of the American brothers. (We always called one another 'brother' and 'sister'.)

How exciting it was to be with so many different people, with different accents, yet all believing the same, talking in the same phraseology! It was all so secure, and all the talk of the end of the world drawing near was not a fearful prospect for we privileged few, but something we looked forward to with a certain smug relish.

I think the thing that mainly concerned me about the coming doom was that my Mum and Dad were to be in the heavenly class of 144,000 and I was to be in the kingdom on earth. There were no ifs or buts about it.

Not that the kingdom on earth was an inferior place. I mean I'd seen pictures of it in the Watchtower books. The lion lying down with the lamb, sunshine and flowers, happy, laughing people. Coupled with my idyllic view of Grandfather's plot, I knew we were in for a good time on earth for sure.

What the group in the heavenlies might be doing was rather obscure, although I had been told they would rule and reign over the earth from their elevated position. They certainly were the elect, not just my Mum and Dad, but the whole 144,000. (You can read about them in the Bible, in Revelation chapter 7, but do read the whole chapter to get the idea in context!)

They were so elect that, when we held the annual memorial service at the Kingdom Hall, only those in this group could partake of the bread and wine. There were very few folk left in my time who qualified for this. Today, in most Kingdom Halls, there are no partakers of the bread and wine, but the memorial service is held once a year and the congregation simply observe the emblems.

Jehovah's Witnesses believe parents should be responsible for teaching their children, bringing them to the meetings and taking them with them on the doors. There are no special groups for children and I had very little opportunity to make friends within the organisation. I used to hope fervently that at the houses we called, there would be children and we would be asked in.

It did happen quite often. Probably the sight of a small, ginger-topped wistful face on their doorstep moved Mums to take pity on me. But I was always told never to go in on my own. It was all very enjoyable. I'd be given a drink and biscuit, and could spend all the time Dad was talking, playing with some newly-acquired friends and their toys. If he was invited back for further visits, I glowed with delight and made a mental note to make sure I was taken along too.

'What's your Dad talking about?' asked a bespectacled young friend one morning.

'About the Bible and that,' I shrugged indifferently, not wanting to be questioned.

'What do you come with him for, then?'

'Oh huh, something to do.'

'Looks pretty boring to me.'

'Not really. Not when you're doing it to earn a place in God's kingdom.' I winced inwardly, afraid of being laughed at.

'Yeah?' He looked more mystified. Then suddenly he said, 'Can you play cards?'

'Cards!' My heart sank, playing cards were forbidden in my home. How could I explain to him such things were of the devil and I dare not touch them! I didn't try to explain. I just said feebly, 'I think I feel sick, I must find my Dad.'

4

INSIDE A KINGDOM HALL

Every Sunday evening we travelled some twenty miles by bus to the Kingdom Hall. Dad was the 'Company Servant' in charge of a congregation of about 100 people.

The hall that we attended must have been at one time a chapel because I recall we sat in pews. This was unusual because frequently Kingdom Halls are hired halls or rented premises, not owned by the Watchtower organisation. Seating was ordinary wooden chairs, in rows it's true, but moveable to create a more friendly informal atmosphere.

These halls are used as planting out places, and in the days when few people had cars, they made the meetings much more accessible to those interested in the area. The halls came in various shapes and sizes as empty shops, community centres, memorial halls were turned into meeting places.

The advantages of using a hired hall were two-fold. First, there were no maintenance costs for the building, and secondly, there was never any danger of people becoming attached to the place sentimentally or seeing it as a sacrosanct 'house of God'. Any Jehovah's Witness is quick to tell a churchgoer that the Bible says: 'God does not dwell in temples made with hands.'

Sunday evenings were given over to the study of the latest Watchtower magazine, which was published bi-monthly. Once again, as in the home Bible studies, the procedure was the question and answer method. Three 'brothers' would sit out front facing the congregation (never a 'sister' out front), one would lead the meeting, another would read the paragraphs from the Watchtower, while everyone would follow his reading from their own copy, and the other brother would read out the questions on each paragraph printed at the bottom of each page.

With the paragraph read aloud and the appropriate question read, the leader would then invite answers from members of the congregation who would raise their hand if they wanted to give the answer.

It was fundamental that answers were always given in the words of the paragraph just read. Anyone who added any ideas of their own, or anything contrary to what was printed in the Watchtower, would not be called upon to answer again. That person would be taken aside afterwards and cautioned about such behaviour. If there was no repentance, he or she would ultimately be disfellowshipped.

The Watchtower study lasted an hour. We would sing a hymn, before and after, from the JW hymn or songbook, the Company Servant would give the announcements and there would be a formal prayer to 'Jehovah God'.

I found Sunday evenings tedious, and my prime occupation during the 'study' was with a drawing pad and pencil. I have no artistic talent but my attempts to draw the brothers out front, with of course some imaginative embellishments such as pointed ears and curly moustaches, often reduced my mother to a delicate state of controlled hysterics.

So with her hankie stuffed to her mouth she sometimes offered to play boxes with me instead, joining up the dots to see who could complete the most. This was safer and no laughing matter, and it was all the same to me so long as it helped to pass the time.

Apart from the people, there is not much to look at in a Kingdom Hall, even if it is an owned building. There are no texts round the walls, no posters, pictures or plaques. All I can remember staring at on Sunday evenings was a banner hung across the front platform which had the words: MORE THAN CONQUERORS THROUGH HIM THAT LOVED US. This was the text for the year designated by the Watchtower Society.

There were doubtless different texts as the years passed, but only this one remains indelibly printed in my mind. How could one be *more* than a conqueror I used to ponder? A conqueror of what, anyway?

I was reluctant to ask anyone to explain because I knew it would mean having to listen to a long spiel, and listening was something I did enough of on Sunday nights anyway.

But one thing was certain, I knew for sure who it was who were more than conquerors. No points if you've guessed as well! Who else but Jehovah's Witnesses? And only them in the whole wide world!

So when I felt like a break from the drawing and the boxes game I would survey the congregation and make my own silent observations.

To see perhaps a certain young man and woman sitting together for the first time, was of great interest. They might eventually marry. How romantic it was and, providing they were both earnest Jehovah's Witnesses everyone would be pleased for them. But if one lagged behind the other, it was I gathered a tricky situation of the 'unequal yoke' and frowned upon.

There was another schoolgirl there, older than me and studious looking. She would even put her hand up to answer the Watchtower questions. I felt inferior, especially as I often sat behind her and viewed with envy her long blonde and curly hair. I sucked a bull's-eye thoughtfully, and wondered how long it would take to grow my spiky ginger mop that length. And would I ever have the nerve to put my hand up in the Watchtower study?

It was difficult to be what people expected of the

Company Servant's daughter, especially as lack of concentration was my forte on Sunday nights. How very serious the people were, most of them, always seeking out my Dad for some earnest conversation after the meeting. I really only liked the people who bothered to talk to me, and to be fair, most of them did and made me feel special and important. But it was my connections in high places that was the reason for that.

Something I did not like at all at the Kingdom Hall we attended, was the presence of two men in wheelchair beds who were wheeled in each Sunday and parked at the front near the platform. They were two brothers, and well I knew that their invalidity had been caused by vaccine damage. It was such a sad spectacle. I could see they were not old men, yet although quite cheerful and smiling, their speech was slurred and hard to understand.

I was not acquainted with suffering in my childhood and the profound sense of disturbance I always felt at the sight of these two brothers has remained through the years. Why, oh why! was my silent cry, but really I did not want an explanation, I wanted not to see them, I wished they were not always there, then I could forget that such people existed.

The people at the Kingdom Hall were very kind and solicitous towards them, but there was never any prayer offered for them, or for anyone who was sick for that matter. There was no teaching on healing, no exposition of the Gospel miracles that might have helped me to learn more about God, his comfort, the meaning of the Cross as well as the promises of Scripture that feed our faith when we are sad and do not understand.

All the people who came to the Kingdom Hall that we opened in a new area came as a direct result of the door-to-door visitation. Many of them I already knew from them having been to the studies taken by my Dad in their homes.

I remember there were two families who lived a few doors away from each other. I had come to know the two children in each family in their homes. Although they lived so near, separate studies were held in each home, for Jehovah's Witnesses aim to make it as easy as possible for husband and wife to study the literature together.

The father of one of the families was a policeman when we first met him. As he and his wife became involved in a 'study' and then began coming to the Watchtower meetings, the next step was to get baptized and go on the doors themselves.

But in order to become a fully-fledged member, it was made clear to him he would have to leave the police force. The Watchtower Society did not approve of anyone being employed in a uniformed occupation which was so much part of this world's corrupt system. Before long he made the choice and gave up his career in the police for a nondescript pen-pushing occupation and became one of the meeting's most zealous workers.

The father of the other family also soon became a zealous worker, but sadly he was stricken with a serious illness and his life could only be saved with a blood transfusion. He had embraced the Watchtower teachings so wholeheartedly that he could not agree to this.

All the conversations I recall overhearing about this man's situation at the time seemed only to reflect on a sense of pride that he had been so strong in faith to refuse this life-saving help. But I also remember seeing, even with a child's eyes, the bewildered look in his wife's eyes and the sadness I felt for the children, younger than me, who were soon to be without their Dad.

His death caused a feeling of intense grief to me, but only for a short time. I thought of him as brave, but wished it had not happened that way. 'Faithful unto death,' they said. I wondered how someone could choose to die when he could have lived. Why was it so important that he didn't 'take blood'?

Jehovah's Witnesses interpret blood transfusions as 'eating blood' and therefore a violation of God's prohibition in the Bible. They base their case on scriptures such as Acts 14:16 and 17:30, 31 which they maintain back up what they say about a law in Genesis 9:3-6 which is relevant for mankind concerning blood. But this law refers to the shedding of blood, that is murder. The expression in Acts to 'abstain from blood' they take as basis for not receiving blood, either in food, or as medicine. The Old Testament laws on animal sacrifices are also referred to in connection with their refusal to 'take blood'.

At no time, when instances such as I have just described occurred, was there ever anything said about prayer for healing for the person in need. Prayer was never important it seemed. We had no family prayers, bedtime prayers or grace before meals, except when we had a pioneer with us.

Life in the Witnesses was all about being on the work, putting in a large number of hours, getting the literature distributed into people's homes, studying the Watchtower diligently and pouring contempt on all who did not see things our way. It was therefore with some surprise, if not incredulity, that I read the following in my autograph book:

> Pray, pray, pray, ever keep on praying.
> In the darkest, dullest day, still his voice obeying.
> Never from the gates of prayer, turn with doubting sorrow.
> For the One who standeth there, may answer thee tomorrow.

The writer was none other than 'Auntie Amy' in whose home we met for 'Bible' study. I was puzzled because nobody ever spoke in those sort of terms about prayer, people were not encouraged to pray. Why then did she write those words? I recall she was ill in bed at the time and did not have long to live. Could it be that, laid aside from all activity, alone often just reading her Bible, she found, or re-found, that personal faith that rests in God alone and needs no props of a man-made organisation? I believe so.

5

INSIDE A CHURCH

My first introduction to a church came when I was nine. It was through my piano teacher, who was also a church organist. I'd been having lessons with Miss Bertha Scott for some time in her front room. The musty smell of an oil stove and the muddle of papers, trinkets and ornaments around the room only contributed to the stuffy, tedious feeling of piano lessons.

As her long bony fingers firmly grasped mine, making me play the right notes with the right timing, the focus of my attention invariably wandered to her pince-nez and the perpetual drop of water on the end of her sharp-pointed nose.

She knew there was something religious about our family, Dad of course had 'witnessed' to her. But she seemed totally unaware of the great gulf fixed between her practice of faith and ours.

'I'm playing the organ for a very big wedding on Saturday. I wondered if you would like to come and watch?' she said benevolently. I gazed up at the tall angular figure, fascinated as ever by the two features of her nose. 'You could come with your friend Vera if you like, I'll mention it to her when she comes for her lesson. You can sit in the gallery where I play the organ and the choirboys will be singing.'

Immediately, the sense of something rather stupid and ridiculous was conjured up in my mind. It would be fun to go with Vera too.

So there we were, Vera and me, perched in the gallery on the opposite side of the organ to the choirboys, peering down on the scene below. Vera had been to a few weddings and was a bit blasé about it all, as expected.

I was nervous about actually being in a church, although it wasn't the awful place I had imagined. It was a modern building, light and bright, and the prettiness of the wedding scene, with bridesmaids dressed in all colours of the rainbow, quite captured my imagination.

I dismissed, as stupid, the attire of the choirboys, and thought the vicar's outfit was laughable. Why did he dress like that? It seemed to me then, even as a child, that he made himself conspicuously different from ordinary people. 'A pompous ass', I'd heard the phrase often, and such seed thoughts, of course, were part of the planting in my life from earliest years.

At our Kingdom Hall the leaders dressed the same as everyone else. They looked like men and spoke in their normal voice when they were out front taking a meeting. I did not like the mystique, the aura, that surrounded the vicar's robed figure. He was only a man, and a deluded one at that! The judgment snapped firmly together in my mind.

Somehow I expected Vera to feel the same, a sort of spooky feeling about that black and white figure with the strange voice. But she didn't seem to treat the spectacle with ridicule or even suppressed giggles.

Vera, of all people, sat there in awe of the vicar and the surroundings. I could see it in her face, and her disapproving glances in my direction made me keep my comments to myself.

But it turned out later that it was, in fact, a superstitious awe that appeared to encapsulate the self-sufficient Vera. She was steeped in superstition of what was lucky and unlucky, and being impolite and giggling about clergymen was one of them. It was in the same category as walking under a ladder or ignoring a black cat.

There was no superstition in me, no awe either. Luck was a worldly expression and consigned by Jehovah's Witnesses to that realm of occult experiences in which, the Bible taught, one was strictly forbidden to dabble.

My second experience of 'church' came soon after this and was again to attend a wedding. The neighbours on either side of our terraced house were not folk that we had a lot to do with, so it was very surprising when Mrs Cramp called over the fence to my Mum one morning, as she hung out the washing, and asked if my sister and me would be bridesmaids at her daughter's wedding.

I'm sure, like Miss Scott, they knew we were religious. My Dad had knocked, more than once, at every house in our street, with the 'message of the kingdom', and one lady had joined the organisation as a result.

But again, like the piano teacher, our neighbours had no awareness of the difference between our kind of religion and that of the Anglican church round the corner.

They labelled us 'religious' - if only they'd known how much that label was hated and despised by followers of the Watchtower Society! The very word 'religious' carried connotations of unspeakable practices, rituals and beliefs surrounded by gloom and darkness, and the destination of all participants was the bottomless pit forever.

Would we be allowed to be bridesmaids at a church wedding? I waited with trepidation for my Dad's reaction. He certainly did not approve, but his heart was soft towards us, his children, and he let us accept the invitation. But he would remain aloof from it all, and certainly not come to the wedding. The involvement was to be entirely my Mother's responsibility.

Excitement began to mount as Mum brought out her old hand-sewing machine onto the table every evening, and began stitching the carefully cut material of pink and peach satin. I thought my pink dress was a dream, with its puffed sleeves and long gathered skirt reaching to my ankles. And when the satin was finally covered with a delicate patterned net, I twirled and twirled with delight in front of the mirror.

I had never worn anything like it before. My entire clothes collection consisted of one school skirt and three blouses, one best winter dress, a few home-knits and home-made summer frocks.

My sister, seven years older than me, was not very excited at all. It was something of an ordeal for her, the thought of being a bridesmaid. Far more reticent and shy, with dark hair, we were not alike in looks or temperament. But Vera was very interested in this important event for her friend Diana, and promised faithfully to be at the church on the day.

The Saturday afternoon arrived eventually and, as we dressed in our finery, Dad walked out the front door, case in hand as usual, to make his door-to-door visits in a neighbouring street.

Feeling utterly splendid and somewhat ethereal, I swept down the front steps and up the other side into the house next door. Then came an unexpected eclipse.

'Jim has brought you both a present for being my bridesmaids,' Irene Cramp, dressed as a bride, spoke with a smile as she bent down to us. 'Look, a beautiful silver cross and chain. One for you and one for you.' She held them out in her hand benevolently.

The world went dark and I stiffened inwardly. I

thought I was going to faint and wished fervently that I might. What should I do? I looked at my mother who seemed to be nonplussed for words. My sister's face registered cold indifference, which was her way of coping.

Coping with what? The very thought of wearing such a symbol of religiosity and idolatry. Those were the words, heard so often, and associated so completely with things like crosses, whatever form they came in.

The argument about the cross is one that is integral in Watchtower teaching. They use terms such as torture stake or tree where Jesus was put to death. They refer to the glorification of the cross as a form of idolatry, along with statues, pictures, relics and stained glass windows. The cross as a symbol of everything religious is spurned and excluded from their thinking.

But there was nothing to be done at this last minute presentation. The bride was fastening the abhorred decoration around my neck. For the time being, all I could do was pretend it wasn't there.

Once back at the wedding reception, I tugged at it, hoping to break it. I succeeded in damaging the clasp and quickly removed it to a place of safety in Mum's handbag. There were a few raised eyebrows and expressions of sorrow that it had broken, but as I didn't appear too distressed, the incident was lost in the ensuing celebrations.

When next-door-but-one neighbour, Mr Tubb, died, his wife took in two Salvation Army ladies as lodgers. This development was discussed with great interest in our house, and there was a lot of laughter about religious fanatics in fancy bonnets. The jaundiced opinions were transferred to my mind immediately.

But I found it hard to reconcile such descriptions with the friendliness and jollity of the girls next-door-but-one. They would always call across the garden with smiling faces and I was attracted to them.

One day they said to my mother, 'Hasn't Diana got a clear singing voice? We heard every word of Ave Maria.'

Mum was understandably a bit mystified by this comment. Where had they heard me singing that religious song? The puzzle was solved when I confessed to enjoying singing sessions while seated in the outside lavatory. And Ave Maria of all things?

Well, I had no idea what or who the song was about. It was just that Vera had the sheet music at her house and I enjoyed playing it on her piano because it had the doh ray me appellations.

Miss Scott, of course, heartily disapproved of using the tonic solfa and insisted I must learn to read music. So I never enlightened her about my ability with Ave Maria.

Vera's Mum said, in a voice oozing with sentimentality, that the song was 'luvely dear'. I could play it and sing to my heart's content on her piano. I must have got carried away in the outside privy, much to the amusement of our neighbours.

But I liked the little 'garden room'. It was a place where I liked to sit for all sorts of reasons besides the obvious.

Grandfather grew his own tobacco for his pipe, and when the leaves had to be dried he put them in this convenient place. They gave off a pleasant aroma. It was cosy too, and warm, with a small oil lamp kept burning continuously and a rag rug on the floor. Most importantly, it had a bolt on the door. I could read or daydream undisturbed.

It wasn't until later on, when we had a bathroom installed with a smart new indoor toilet, that I saw that outside hermitage as the bleak and primitive closet it really was.

Sometimes the Salvation Army band would play in our street. As we sat behind the net curtains in the front room, Mum with her sewing, Nan with her eyes peeled for anything or anyone that moved outside, ridicule was rife, and Dad dismissed the Salvation Army as a 'load of poppycock'.

'But they're ever so nice!' I complained. 'Why don't you like them?'

'It's not the people, Diana, I don't like, it's the system, the religious system. That's what's wrong, corrupted, and the people are trapped in it, deceived by the leaders who are just humbugs.'

Sadly I turned away, but clung to his admission that at least he liked the people. 'And so do I, so do I,' I thought.

6

STILL DIFFERENT

I had been just a few weeks at the Grammar School when the gym teacher asked me to stay behind while the rest of the class left the room. I had a feeling what was coming.

She spoke kindly but firmly, 'Diana, you are the only one in this class who has not had any vaccinations. Would you please ask your parents if they would reconsider their decision and give their permission?'

'Yes, Miss West,' said I obediently, but I knew they would not consent.

'What did Westy want?' clamoured three girls waiting in the corridor.

'Nothing much, about vaccinations, I haven't had any.'

'Why not?' demanded Sandra Tucker. Her curious gaze was not kind.

'My parents don't agree with it.'

'Oh, they'd rather you caught TB or polio instead, I suppose?'

'No, they believe it's wrong to transfer blood in any way.'

'What, even to save life?'

‘Are you a Catholic or something?’ chipped in Brenda.

‘Don’t be daft, Bren! Catholics get vaccinated, it’s contraception they don’t agree with.’

Sandra looked pleased at the smirks on one or two faces. True to form she had made the popular, amusing comment.

As we wandered out to the playground I felt bothered. I knew I ought to have explained more, and told my friends I was in the Jehovah’s Witnesses and proud of it.

But at that moment I didn’t feel proud at all of my religious pedigree, just plain fed up at always being made to feel different from others. At secondary school the conflicts were becoming sharper as more of the world opened up, and increasingly I questioned inwardly the strange and different lifestyle I had always known.

All my life I had known security in belonging to an organisation. Now as my world became enlarged, I wanted to exchange that security for another, and that was to be the same as everybody else.

Our Sunday evening bus ride to the Kingdom Hall now contained a new dimension for me. The bus route passed right by Olga’s house.

Olga was our form captain, and I’d developed a bit of a schoolgirl’s crush on her. She was tall, dark and athletic - how I wished I was! She knew a lot of poetry and even wrote verse. Anyone who wrote had the power of a magnet for me even then. Olga was far more mature and composed for her thirteen years than anyone else in the form, and she was very popular. My feelings towards Olga bothered me, particularly when there was a serious example at school of where such things led.

Nina was a girl in the fourth year who flung herself down in front of a teacher's car one morning as she drove into school.

'She had a crush on Miss Jones,' they said. 'Just idolized her, always following her round the school ...', so the gossip went on amongst the girls and I listened soberly. Nina had not been fatally injured, but she was absent from school for a long time afterwards and the gossip went on - 'A bit loopy, mental' were the unkind comments.

I thought about Nina, reflecting on her rather babyish expression, her peculiar mannerisms, her nervous apologetic way of speaking. She had a nymph-like quality, ethereal not-of-this-world look. And there was Miss Jones, a geography teacher, strong, lively, persuasive, a leader among women, enthusing vitality and confidence.

When Nina cast herself down before her and nearly lost her life, I thought I understood. The same emotional power surged through me at times. But it was my secret and I wanted to keep it that way.

So I satisfied the emotional pull on Sunday evenings by sitting on the right-hand side of the bus going and the left-hand side coming back. As it drew up at the bus stop I could peer almost into Olga's front room, in breathless anticipation of catching a glimpse of my idol. Sadly I never did get even a glimpse, but for the rest of the journey I was lost in a daydream of Olga and me talking and laughing together, a fantasy world where we were best friends forever.

At the Watchtower meeting such fantasies had no place, no future, and never could I tell Olga about Jehovah's Witnesses. The two involvements were worlds apart and I felt guilty about my secret. I felt there was something wrong about it, but I couldn't help my feelings.

No doubt, the guilt was due to an absorbed sense of morality from my earliest years, for Jehovah's Witnesses are very moral in their lives and in their relationships. Strong teaching is given in the Watchtower on this area. There is no excuse for sexual perversion, dishonesty, adultery; there are no grey areas. If things are wrong according to the Bible then they must be shunned by a servant of Jehovah God.

Co-habitation would never be condoned, inordinate affection is out, along with smoking and 'wine-bibbing', as they would call it. Public houses are no places to be found in, neither are gambling dens, the betting turf or nudist beach.

Modesty in a woman's dress is emphasized, but they are not peculiar in their dress at all. They make no insistence on long hair and hats for women or no make-up. Neither are they dowdy, dull or attention-drawing by their outward appearance. They look clean, wholesome and healthy, and their lives are so.

If the teaching given by the organisation is not adhered to, that person will not be allowed to attend a Kingdom Hall.

At secondary school I attended the daily assembly and religious instruction lessons. I believe my parents thought these were innocuous, of none effect, and they were right. I adopted a very cynical, superior attitude to it all, dismissing as 'not what I believe' anything that was said. Only Bible readings I could listen to with approval.

When the headmistress read that 'whatsoever' passage in Philippians 4:8: 'Whatsoever things are true, honest, just, whatsoever things are pure, whatsoever things are lovely, whatsoever things are of good report; if there be any virtue, and if there be any praise, think on these things', there was always a few smirks passed between the members of 3A. And Sandra Tucker always seemed to take issue with me about such words.

I felt nervous of Sandra, wary of her sharp tongue and sly insinuations. She often tried to rile me. I was so different from her, and my home-life was sheltered and quaint by comparison. She couldn't be blamed for being a product of her environment as I was of mine.

But I felt uncomfortable, out-of-place whenever I went to her home. I found her mother overpowering with her noisy raucous laugh, her unabashed use of swear words, blasphemies and vulgar jokes. I knew the pub and the club were where her parents spent their spare time.

Sandra was clever, with a quick mind. She could get better marks than me in exams, even though I silently appealed to Jehovah God for help. She possessed the power of intimidation over those she thought were goody-goodies. But it was people like Mr and Mrs Tucker who at least made me feel very grateful for my own parents and the way they were so different.

School assemblies sometimes raised problems for me with the hymns we sang, most especially those that mentioned the word 'Trinity'. 'Holy, holy, holy, Lord God Almighty ... God in three persons, blessed Trinity ...'. I always stopped short at this line and would not, could not, sing the words.

I really did not understand what the argument was all about, but I knew it was basic to Jehovah's Witness belief that one did not accept the idea of the Trinity. The church doctrine of the Trinity is in fact their chief target of attack. They point out that the word is not to be found in the Bible, which makes it suspect for a start.

What visions filled my head at the very mention of the word! In the words of a Watchtower publication, *Let God Be True*: 'Sincere persons who want to know the true God and serve Him find it a bit difficult to love and worship a complicated, freakish-looking, three-headed God.'

I was taught the doctrine of the Trinity originated with Satan and that thc 'mystery of iniquity' mentioned in Scripture referred to it. The Watchtower teaching is that Christ did have a part in creation, but only after the Father had first created him. And that Christ in his pre-human existence was Michael the archangel.

But visions of a three-headed god and such like would float around in my head at the sight or sound of the word 'Trinity'. And while the rest of the school sung on oblivious, I struggled with that picture in my head, and the doorstep debates I had listened to for so long, and could not sing any more.

However, I learned to handle assemblies without too much concern. They were easily dismissed as the school day began in earnest. That is until a new headmistress came on the scene.

We had got used to Miss Jewel-Hunt and appreciated her smart appearance and habit of wearing something different each day, plus a good smattering of make-up. One could focus on her with interest every assembly morning, and what she said with her voice did not speak to us half as much as what she was wearing. We were sorry she had to leave us, for some trendy school in America, so the story went.

She was a thoroughly Modern Millie, the stuff that schoolgirls in uniform dream about for themselves, one day.

The new headmistress walked down the aisle of upstanding girls to the front dais. We stared in dismay at her comparatively plain dress and pulled back hairstyle. Nothing very interesting here. We waited for the usual 'Good morning girls' before being seated, but it never came. Instead we heard a clear and pleasant voice say with feeling, 'God bless you all'.

Back in the form room there was a buzz about Miss Watson and a lot of mockery from some as they mimicked her opening words. I felt uneasy. Part of me wanted to join in the mockery and part of me wanted to stick up for her. She was obviously one of those religious hypocrites, and as such an object of ridicule, according to my book. But I could not stand the sneering tone of Sandra Tucker and I didn't really want to be identified with her. Perhaps Miss Watson had only said that because it was her first morning, and tomorrow we would return to normal. But no, every morning now began with those four words.

'Bless us all, bless us all, the long and the short and the tall,' hooted Sandra and friends. I said nothing, but noticing other girls who were ignoring the jibes and sarcasm I felt drawn towards them.

Before long I discovered that Rosemary, Maureen,

Eileen and Lorna belonged to the Salvation Army. My previous attraction to the Salvation Army ladies who had lived in our street, stood me in good stead as I veered toward these girls, almost wishing I could be one of them. At least they had each other to share their beliefs with. I was alone with my strange background.

I remember vividly the day when Lorna's Dad died suddenly. It so happened he worked with my Grandfather in the blacksmith's shop of the Royal Arsenal Cooperative Society in Woolwich. It was there at work that he collapsed and died one morning.

But Lorna, who went home at dinner time with her three friends and discovered the sad news, returned to school that afternoon as usual. As Rosemary sat with her arm around her, in the English lesson, and I sat behind them both, I wondered how she could be so calm and composed. How could Lorna possibly carry on as if nothing had happened?

I had the feeling that it was somehow to do with the Salvation Army. Could it be alright to belong to them? Could there be an exception here? After all they were not really religious like church people. They didn't have big gloomy buildings and droning vicars.

Grandfather thought very highly of them too and gave them money when they knocked at our door. 'They're alright, duck, do a lot of good and help the poor,' he would tell me. But then Grandfather wasn't a Jehovah's Witness.

I felt Lorna and her friends had something more than I had. I knew that if my Dad died suddenly I'd be devastated, distraught, lost. All my head knowledge of the Bible and all my Jehovah's Witness indoctrination would not have prepared me for such a tragedy.

Instinctively, I knew that whatever it was that Lorna had, it was connected with the Salvation Army somehow. One day I would find that elusive something and my instincts were proved right. But until then the influence of people and events would continue to make indelible marks on my memory in the growing-up years.

7

AWAY FROM HOME

A new girl had joined the form and what's more she lived in my road. So it was natural enough to strike up a friendship with Erica as we began travelling to and from school together. Erica was quiet and studious with serious grey eyes.

I was impressed by her attitude to schoolwork, mine being so much more casual and flippant even at times. And Erica was good at everything, not only academic subjects; she could draw, sing, sew and cook. Her prowess on the sports field, at the swimming pool and in the gym left me standing in awe.

I envied her for all these abilities, and although we became friends, it was only because we lived so near each other. I doubt it would have happened for any other reason. Erica was on another plane altogether, I liked and admired her, but her quiet reserve was a mystery to me. There seemed to be an unhappiness about her which I could not fathom. What had she got to be unhappy about with all those gifts and talents?

Erica never talked much about her home and family. I knew her Mum went out to work which was unusual. All the Mums I knew were at home all day.

And that she had a younger brother and sister. Then at Christmas time something happened.

I knocked on Erica's door one Saturday morning, with a homework problem. She would have the answer, I knew for sure.

Her father opened the door. 'Come on in and have a drink,' he insisted.

Thinking in terms of lemonade I went in happily enough, only to be presented with a large glass of dark red strong-smelling liquid. I was too nervous to refuse this rather strange man. He poured Erica a glass and kept saying, 'Drink it up, do you good, Happy Christmas!'

I drank it up quickly and Erica's Mum came in just as I was draining the tumbler. She looked very embarrassed. 'You shouldn't have given her all that port wine,' she looked angrily at her husband.

Erica just stood there saying nothing.

Mr Edwards had a funny smile on his face. He was in fact looking altogether funny, as if he couldn't stand up properly. He gave a short laugh at his wife and left the room.

I excused myself hurriedly and walked down the road home wondering why the familiar privet hedges looked so peculiar and unreal. My head was spinning and I had to grab hold of the garden walls to get myself home.

'Whatever's the matter with you?' I felt Mum staring at me as I staggered in the front door.

'I feel sick ... and giddy. Erica's Dad gave me a drink, port wine, a big glassfull. Said it'd do me good.'

'Erica's Dad!' exclaimed Mum. 'What a thing to do!'

I could explain no more as Mum propelled me to the bathroom.

That was the only encounter I ever had with Mr Edwards. He was always a vague, spectre-like figure in the background, it seemed. He never came to school concerts or parents' evenings.

Of course, I didn't talk about my Dad much to Erica or to anyone else. I knew my friends would think he was strange as well as religious. But after that nauseating glass of port wine, I reckoned that an hour's Watchtower study on Sunday was a lot easier to live with. I just felt sorry for Erica.

Miss Jones walked out of the classroom, leaving a buzz of excitement behind her.

'Will you go? Would you like to?' we asked one another eagerly. Miss Jones had just told us there was to be a school trip to Switzerland in the summer.

'Switzerland!' gasped Pam with a mock faint. 'Just think of all those snowcapped mountains and shimmering lakes.'

'And pine-clad forests and milk chocolate,' I added.

'And the yodellers,' mused Erica.

‘For a whole fortnight without parents,’ chipped in Janice.

Lorna and her friends sat quietly listening to our furore of imagination.

‘Do you think you will go?’ I asked hopefully.

Lorna shook her head wistfully, ‘No, I’m sure my Mum couldn’t afford it.’

‘Nor mine,’ agreed her friend Rosemary.

Afford it! That hadn’t occurred to me. It was, I suppose, a lot of money. I might not be able to go either.

Sandra was not the least bit interested. ‘Who wants to go on holiday with the school!’ she sneered. ‘You’ll have to wear school uniform every day and walk in a crocodile, and be in bed by nine o’clock probably.’

She grinned slyly at our crestfallen faces and, pausing only to moisten her thick lips, added, ‘I’d rather go to Margate with my Mum and Dad. It’s more fun than being with stuffy old schoolteachers. And we can stay up until midnight at the club.’

Her friend Joanne nodded agreeably. ‘Yeah, it was good last year, wasn’t it, Sandie? I can’t wait to go again and see those boys, remember?’ She winked at Sandra.

Erica looked torn. Sandra’s out-of-school exploits always seemed to fascinate her. But then she suddenly railed on them. ‘But Switzerland’s much more exciting than Margate, and we won’t have to wear school uniform all the time anyway. You can go to Margate any time.'

Sandra shook her head firmly. 'No, I don't want to go.'

A flood of relief surged through me. I certainly didn't want Sandra to go either. And from what I'd heard about that Margate holiday she was welcome to go back again, Jo as well.

The next morning I knocked for Erica as usual.

'Can you go?' I asked eagerly.

'I think so, what about you?'

'I think so, although it's a lot of money for my Mum and Dad to find. I suppose it's easier for you because your Mum goes to work.'

'Hmm, in some ways,' she spoke hesitatingly. 'I don't know if my father will pay anything. He might do it for my brother but not for me.'

I glanced at her sympathetically. My Mum and Dad always treated my sister and me the same, there was never any favouritism, even though my sister kept away from the Jehovah's Witnesses meetings and now, being a nurse, lived away from home.

Erica's Mum was a very nice cheery person who soon confirmed she was willing to let Erica go to Switzerland, and that settled my present concern.

When it was finally agreed that I also could go my appreciation for my parents knew no bounds. I vowed I'd be grateful to them forever. I didn't tell them, but I had feared secretly that the confines of my 'religious' upbringing would prevent my being allowed to go. But the fact it was under the auspices of the school made it more acceptable I'm sure. It could be classed as an educational trip.

At the time I had no idea of the tremendous upheaval my parents were soon to be embroiled in. Their restlessness and inner uncertainty had not been communicated to me. With the eyes of youth I looked only superficially at them anyway, and saw no indication of anything amiss.

But that was all to come, after Switzerland. Nothing else occupied my thinking, dreaming and imagination in the months leading up to August.

A school dance was arranged with the local boys' school at the end of the summer term. I was reluctant to go, but afraid of being labelled 'different' if I stayed away. I hated the occasion and I couldn't dance.

But Erica could and had spent all evening gliding across the floor with some gawky-looking sixth-former, just as if she always did that sort of thing.

It dawned on me that evening that Erica's life out of school was a blank page to me, as I suppose mine was to her. But she told me how she went to what she called 'socials' on a Saturday night at the Co-op hall. Her Mum went and had started taking Erica with her, and that's how she'd learned to dance. I also discovered she went to a tennis club on Sundays.

Dimly I was beginning to realise Erica knew a lot

about things I didn't. She'd had experiences out there in the world from which I'd been so sheltered.

There'd been the make-up incident too.

'What's all that stuff plastered on your face?' I'd exploded with shock, after bumping into Erica unexpectedly one Saturday afternoon.

'Make-up,' she'd said calmly, 'why don't you wear it?'

Chance would be a fine thing, I thought, but said breezily, 'I don't like it, it looks a mess'.

That was a lie. Erica was transformed with bright pink lipstick, rouged cheeks and glistening long eyelashes. But I could just hear my Mum saying, 'Dolled up to the nines she was, I wouldn't like to catch you looking like that!'

'Those boys over there are going too. Their luggage labels are the same as ours, School Journey Association, Einsiedeln, Switzerland.'

I followed Erica's interested gaze at the gaggle of boys standing along the station platform. They were in school uniform like us. Glancing back at Erica's face I noticed her eyes had lost their usually serious look and were sort of animated. 'Those boys ...', her words plopped like stones into a pool and I felt ripples of anxiety spreading out inside me. And I remembered I'd felt the same at the school dance.

On the train to London, sitting with Erica, Pam, Janice and Ann that August morning, I knew that being away from home on this school holiday, it would be difficult to be different from the others.

The whole Jehovah's Witness thing would, therefore, have to be pushed to one side. It just would not exist for the next two weeks as far as I was concerned. I wanted to be like everyone else, be one of them, a fifteen-year-old schoolgirl, like the girls I was travelling with. Well, there would be no difference I decided. I could enjoy what they enjoyed and forget for two whole weeks all the things that made me feel so different.

On the train to Dover I began to relax. We were moving now fast to new places, new experiences. Nothing was going to matter except enjoying myself.

The Channel crossing over, the long journey overnight by train began. The most comfortable way to sleep, we discovered, was in the luggage rack of the compartment. Laughing, we arranged a rota, each spending an hour on the rack in turn while the others catnapped on the slatted wooden seats, or stood in the corridor chatting excitedly as the train sped through the night.

The adventure had begun.

'Einsiedeln,' said Pam, reading from the information sheet we'd been given, 'is, after Rome and Lourdes, the most celebrated pilgrimage centre in Europe. It lies 2,895 feet above sea level between the valleys of the Sihl and Alp ...'.

'Shut up, I'm trying to sleep!' complained Janice.

But Pam was wide awake after her hour in the luggage rack and droned on, 'St Meinrad was the first ...' .

Vaguely as Pam's voice floated through my subconscious, words like - pilgrimage, monk, monastery, cathedral - stabbed me with concern. I didn't remember reading that. It sounded like a lot of dead religion and superstitious humbug.

Still I wasn't going to let that bother me. I was on my way to Switzerland, land of snowcapped mountains, pine-clad hills, picturesque wooden chalets. I set this scene firmly in my mind to blot out what Pam was saying. Yet she wasn't saying it in a very religious way. She was really making fun of it and I could join in happily on that. Making fun of anything religious was home ground for me.

'Welcome to Drei Kônigen.' The proprietors of the hotel gave us a warm reception.

And it was a picture-book setting that confronted us. A white painted chalet, wooden shutters and window boxes of colourful flowers, hanging baskets with trailing plants, standing in the blaze of brilliant sunshine. We could only gasp with pleasure at the thought of staying here for two whole weeks.

'Drei Kônigen, that's three kings,' commented Pam knowledgeably. 'Probably the ones that came to Bethlehem in the Christmas story.'

Others nodded but I did not. Three kings? I remembered we'd sung carols in assembly and Erica had sung a solo, that's right she was one of the kings, 'Myrrh is mine its bitter perfume ...'. I remembered those words because Erica's voice had been so strong and clear. None of us knew she could sing like that and afterwards lots of people told her what a lovely voice she had.

Yes, three kings, the connection was dawning. But the Christmas story, as Pam referred to it, well that was just a piece of religious poppycock to my mind. The facts had got all twisted up with pagan traditions. Who said they were kings? The Bible said 'wise men' and it didn't say how many either. I'd been told they were probably astrologers, stargazers.

Christmas time in my home was a secular affair. A happy time with presents and special food but no tree or decorations, and no realisation at all on my part of what Christmas celebrated. Listening on the doorsteps I'd gleaned it was really a big farce, even the date was wrong. Some Witnesses made a point of going out on the doors on Christmas morning, to demonstrate their indifference to the occasion.

Anyway, here I was in this Three Kings Hotel; never mind the name, it was a wonderful place to be. I shared a room in the front with Ann and Erica.

Looking from our window we could see across the village square to the great monastery building with its large clock face and bell tower. Around the square there were gaily decorated market stalls. We couldn't wait to explore.

On our single beds were lovely soft duvets, an unknown feature in English bedrooms at that time.

Pam and Janice burst in to look at our room, they were across the landing. 'Have you seen Betsie and Freda yet?'

'Who are you talking about?'

'They're on the landing. Come and see,' they said mysteriously.

The toilets were on the landing between our rooms, and Pam gleefully showed us the door-locks which registered the German words for 'engaged' and 'vacant' - betzetest and frieda. And that settled things for good. We never went to the toilet, lavatory or loo, we paid visits to Freda or waited outside Betsie.

'Where are the boys staying?' It was Ann who asked Miss Jones the million dollar question.

'Down the road to the station. But you are not to go to their hotel, and they are not to come here!' she warned.

We would be obedient. It was more than our holiday was worth to break the rules or upset Miss J. After breakfast next morning she reiterated the rules for the benefit of others from fifth and sixth years.

As well as the no-go area of the boys' hotel she

warned us about behaviour in 'this friendly pilgrimage centre'. We were not to wander outside the village, we were to be polite, courteous and quiet at all times. There would be trips to Lucerne and Mount Rigi, and evening get-togethers in the monastery hall. She suggested we kept our limited pocket money to spend in the larger towns where things would be cheaper.

Pocket money was indeed limited. Most of our parents had scraped and sacrificed for us to come to Switzerland. A limit had been imposed so we all had the same amount. But it didn't cost anything to browse, and once breakfast was over we were out into the sunshine exploring the village, the shops and the market stalls.

'How revolting!' I recoiled inwardly at the clutter of ornate crucifixes and images, souvenirs, shrines and rosaries, candles and pictures, the religious trash and trinkets. I certainly wouldn't be spending any money here. But neither would any of my friends, judging by their whispered comments.

Apple-faced elderly women, dressed in black, sat benignly by their stalls but we turned away, and seeing the price of a bar of chocolate, remembered Miss Jones' warning and bought nothing.

On the second day at Einsiedeln, Erica and Pam, who had wandered off by themselves for a walk, returned with excitement.

'We've met some really good-looking Swiss

boys!' they enthused. 'They live down the village and they've asked us to go for a walk with them. There's a path *á la croix*. A couple of them speak French and if we go up the hill you can see over the whole village ...'.

The words tumbled out and their enthusiasm was infectious.

'What's á la croix?' I demanded.

'Oh there's a cross with seats round it. Come with us tomorrow night.'

Paul, Herman and Walter were waiting outside Drei Kônigen the next evening. Erica, I noticed, had put on some make-up, and after the evening meal we slipped out of the hotel. There were no restrictions on going out for a walk if there was nothing organised for the evening.

'A la croix', as Pam referred to our destination, was I gathered quite a focal point in the village. But I was totally unprepared for the impact that trysting place was to have on me during that first evening visit.

As we followed the winding path to the top of the hill, we came suddenly into a clearing, dominated by a huge crucifix with a figure on it. I felt frightened, for it seemed to tower over us with awesome effect. And people were sitting on the seats around this monstrosity, unaware, unaffected it seemed by the agonised expression of the figure on the cross.

I reeled inwardly with an even stronger sense of

revulsion and thought, 'This is religion at its worst.' There was no connection, no association in my mind with the ideas, the teaching, I had inherited. It seemed the epitome of the gloom, joylessness and ornate hypocrisy of the religious establishment in this world. Such phrases ran readily through my mind.

And the pious-looking women sitting there. What a dreary and dark religion they adhered to! They were prisoners of a terrible ritualistic system. I shuddered and turned my back on the great cross.

Were these Swiss boys religious then, I wondered? They seemed totally unconcerned about the surroundings, unaffected by the sombre presence of this crucifix, as did my schoolfriends.

Before long others, from the other school parties staying in Einsiedeln, joined us and we met Kevin and Dave, Eddie and John. We laughed and joked and swapped stories of our adventures so far.

Pam whispered to me, 'Kevin is Betty Webb's boyfriend.'

'Betty! In our class?'

Pam nodded. 'She told me Kevin was coming and hoped he wouldn't find another girlfriend.'

I glanced over to where Kev was talking with Ann and Janice. He was tall and good-looking, with brown curly hair and a loud friendly laugh. He seemed to be very interested in Ann, looking down at her with one foot on the seat where she sat. It looked to me as if he'd always known her.

Back in our bedrooms that night, 'which one do you fancy?' was the subject. Erica was keen on Walter, Janice swooned about Herman, Pam was all for John Jacques. Ann refused to be drawn about Kev but he had spent most of the evening with her.

'And what about you, Diana, who do you like? Dave was looking at you a lot, didn't you notice?'

No, I hadn't noticed, I'd been too bothered about that awful crucifix. But, of course, they'd never believe I'd not been thinking about the boys we met that night. 'I like Eddie,' I declared.

'Eddie!' they chorused, 'he's a skinny shrimp.'

'He's good-looking,' I countered. But what I really meant was he looked just like Douglas at the Kingdom Hall. That's what attracted me. But no-one was going to drag that out of me.

For the rest of the holiday I think I managed to be like my friends and put aside my inbred attitudes and reactions to the religious environment of Einsiedeln. Dave became friendly and we paired off, which helped me not to feel so different from the others. Home seemed worlds away, and the days were full of exciting new experiences. It was easy to enter in to it all and forget life as it was in England, in South-East London, and in the Jehovah's Witnesses.

8

GOODBYE TO JEHOVAH GOD

'Forty-love!' shouted Dave slamming a tennis ball viciously over the net at me.

'Watch out!' warned Erica, 'he's mad with you.'

'What, because we're winning?'

'No, silly. I think it's because you won't go out with him.'

Tennis had been the order of the day, ever since we returned from Switzerland. Usually it was Erica and me, Dave and John. But apart from that I wanted nothing to do with Dave. He didn't seem the same as he was on holiday.

Nothing in fact seemed the same any more. I knew I had changed too. Being away from home had opened up new vistas. And the sheltered and secure framework of my home and the Watchtower organisation seemed more like prison walls from which there was no immediate hope of escape.

I had one more year at school when hopefully I'd be allowed to leave, and take a Pitman's College course in shorthand and typewriting. Then all I longed to do was get a job as a journalist. I'd be independent and free to live life to the full.

At the Kingdom Hall there was an air of unease.

I overheard something of the serious conversations people were having with Dad, of disagreements with what the Watchtower Society was saying. There were rumblings and murmurings amongst people which I'd never been aware of before. Several 'brothers' were coming over from the American headquarters at this time, and ideas and structures were changing. Dad was no longer the Company Servant in charge. There were clashes of personality.

But the main expression of disagreement emerged during the Watchtower study evenings. In answering the questions from the read passage, Dad would reply in his own words instead of repeating the printed phrases. He also added ideas of his own which deviated from the text. This was deliberately conflicting and disturbing, and soon his arm raised to answer a question was ignored.

The situation could not be tolerated for long and in a matter of weeks, after returning from Switzerland, Mum calmly told me we would not be going to the Kingdom Hall any more, or going on the door-to-door work.

I felt too stunned to ask questions, or even to talk about it all. It was unbelievable that my parents had left the Jehovah's Witnesses after thirty years of such intense involvement. I just couldn't understand what it was all about.

What I did understand though, and very quickly, was what this would mean for me. It meant I would be free at weekends, on Sundays, to do what I pleased. The whole framework of my life had gone and there was nothing to replace it. Nothing religious that is. For how could I turn to a church after all I had been led to believe about those establishments?

All in all, things couldn't have happened at a better time. At fifteen, with an awakening of new relationships, an awareness of boys as possibly offering exciting new things, I was glad to be free of the past, the restrictions of Jehovah God and his organisation at last. I certainly did not need to feel different any more. I was like Erica, Pam and all the others. A whole new world beckoned and gladly I followed.

Mum and Dad took to going out for walks on Sundays. They seemed closer, contented and even more companionable than they'd ever been. So my security at home was unthreatened. I still had a firm and loving base from which to try out my wings of independence. Release from the Jehovah's Witness organisation gave me a passport into the 'far country' whose delights I had only heard about and never had the chance to sample.

But it was not without some disturbance of mind that these things were realised. With the new freedom, the old boundaries of belief and behaviour were swept away, and that over-riding sense of purpose banished. The faith I had been brought up with was centred in an organisation whose work and teaching filled our lives. I could not automatically throw off the years, and the most formative years of my life at that, without some qualms, fears and apprehensions.

The fact that my parents had apparently thrown off everything, I found confusing. They said nothing, explained nothing to me of how they felt and thought. No doubt, they were in a greater state of disturbance than I was, but they kept it to themselves. My sister was out of all this, living away from home, and my ageing grandparents made no comment to me about the shattering turn of events.

In reality, I could not throw off everything, discard the past, as much as I wanted to. There was nothing to put on instead. And to be stripped of all belief would have left me feeling deeply insecure. So I did the alternative, I buried everything.

Right down under the surface it all went, everything I had ever believed, and I began to pile on top all the pleasures and self-satisfactions of this life. I was free to please myself without incurring the wrath of Jehovah God, for I had to bury this image along with the rest. And in my heart I said 'there is no God'.

Almost at a stroke the parting took place. Watchtower magazines disappeared from the house, along with books and booklets we'd studied and hiked round the doors over the years.

There were others who also left the organisation at this time. The Watchtower Society was no longer the Truth and Dad kept in touch with these people and met together with them for Bible study in their homes. Thankfully, I was not expected to go.

One year on, Pam wrote in my autograph book: 'If all the boys lived over the sea, what a wonderful swimmer Diana would be'. Enough said!

It was an exhilarating time, especially as the day of leaving school approached. My years of homework had finished and I determined not to spend one evening indoors. I planned to join an amateur dramatic society, enrol for evening classes, go out with John, or whoever, and not allow time for one dull moment, or to feel fed up or wonder just where it was all leading. I could hardly wait to get launched. To get free of home as much as possible.

But one Monday morning I received a timely jolt to my aspirations. I knocked at Erica's door as usual, but there was no answer. All day long I wondered where she was.

As soon as I arrived home I sensed my mother knew something by the tone of her question. 'Was Erica at school today?'

'No, there was no answer this morning.'

'Mrs Roberts across the road told me her father collapsed in the street last night and an ambulance was called! She says she thinks he'd tried to commit suicide because Erica's mother has left him.'

‘Where’s Erica?’

‘She’s gone too, and her brother and sister. Of course, Mrs Roberts might have got it wrong. She is a gossip and how she finds out about these things is a bit peculiar.’

The word ‘peculiar’ was carefully chosen and pronounced. I knew why. Mrs Roberts attended a spiritualist meeting.

Suddenly I felt ashamed of how I’d tossed aside as ‘restrictive’ and ‘boring’ my secure home and loving parents. I knew instead it was comfortable, secure, and different. I felt glad it had always been so.

The next day Erica returned to school, although she never came back to live in our street. She stayed at her grandmother’s house. And she never spoke of what had happened until, many years later, when we both became Christians.

9

THEY ARE DIFFERENT

I sat nervously in front of an efficient lady interviewer.

'You may start work here next Monday,' she said.

'Thank you,' I replied and made to leave.

'Oh, just one thing I might mention,' she added. 'You will find the girls who work here rather different from the usual sort of office girl. You'll see.'

She smiled as my face registered startled curiosity. And with that I was ushered out.

My interview for a first job was successfully over. At seventeen it was an important occasion. But just how important it was I did not then dream. In fact, if anyone could have told me the significance of that occasion, or what that parting remark referred to, it is doubtful I would have turned up on the following Monday morning.

But I had no idea of what was ahead, and as to how the girls might be different I didn't imagine, and wasn't a great deal concerned. My head was full of my own ideas, my own plans and aspirations, full of myself.

On Monday morning I was packed off from home

with a good breakfast and various admonitions about busy London roads and friendly gentleman strangers. My grandmother called out, 'If you don't like it come home.'

That, I determined, was the very last thing I would do. Having been launched from the nest, I was going to stay airborne all by myself. Even if there were fears within and lack of confidence, those things could be camouflaged.

It was lunch-break on the very first day of my very first job, when the self-bubble on which I floated got its first prick. In between munching sandwiches and reading a woman's magazine, I glanced over to the girl at the desk opposite.

Ruth Flowerday had been sitting there all morning working hard and there had been little conversation. I'd summed her up by her appearance as dull and serious, and not my type. She was also munching and reading, but my mouth went dry as I saw the book on her desk. There was no mistaking it. It was a Bible.

A feeling of annoyance surged through me - reading a Bible in the office - she must be one of those pious religious types and a two-faced hypocrite into the bargain.

My buried past rose up in indignation. All religious people were hypocrites. They went to church, as if that did them any good, but under the guise of 'church' they indulged in such things as dancing, whist drives, garden fêtes and moneymaking bazaars.

There was no whole-hearted dedication to what they believed. They didn't go from door to door like we did. They didn't deny themselves any pleasures and live according to God's laws, like we did. Hypocrites through and through most of them.

And the vicars in charge were just blind leaders of the blind, duping the people, deceiving their minds. They did not have the Truth, wolves in sheep's clothing most of them. But Jehovah God would vindicate his name one day, utter destruction was their portion.

Wait a minute! Hadn't I dispensed with all that. What did it matter now, it was a thing of the past and I didn't believe in anything any more?

Sitting in the office, only now pretending to read the woman's magazine, I felt all this eruption inside me and knew that all I had been taught to believe was still very much part of me. It was still an inner conviction although I no longer conformed outwardly.

It was ingrained in my thinking, my attitudes just as it always had been for I had never known anything else. There had been no Sunday School in my life, never a church service, no associations with any form of youth club or church-connected activity. No long contact at all with people outside of Jehovah's Witnesses. It had been my way of life since birth. Much of it was still my way of thought.

The realisation of this came as a tremendous

shock, but I said nothing to Bible-reading Ruth. I'll wait, I thought smugly, until she actually says something, commits herself with words, and then I'll explode her ideas for her.

How could she sit there so piously reading a Bible which she couldn't possibly understand anyway without the Watchtower literature to help? And she didn't look as if she could say 'boo to a goose'. You had to be militant to be effective.

So the first day passed.

It was even more disconcerting the next day when Ruth sat there again engrossed in her Bible. Was she going to do this every day?

Feeling very prickly inside I suddenly burst out, 'Ruth, would you like to borrow my *Woman's Own*? I've finished with it.'

She looked up, smiled politely and took it with murmured thanks. But I noticed she only gave it a flick through and then she was back to that Bible.

I felt thoroughly aggravated. Having been brought up to study the Bible I ought perhaps to have felt pleased, or at least interested, to see someone enjoying reading it in their lunch-hour. But I didn't believe anyone could make sense of it without the Watchtower study aids, so I concluded she was putting on a pious act. Also, I was in the land of the rebellious and it was most annoying to be reminded of anything religious.

What's more I felt that sooner or later something

would be said and I should have to divulge my background. I was not ashamed of it, just fed up with it and did not want to get involved. There seemed too many complications and inwardly I was in a mess. To bury it all and live life to the full was the only safe policy I could think of.

That meant a full programme of pleasure, a mad noisy whirl which left no time to think. Theatres, dances, tennis on Sundays, all tasted that much more delicious because they had been forbidden fruit. Fashion, make-up and boyfriends completed the picture. But it was really a protective camouflage, keeping the tangled real self hidden from the light.

But before that first week at work was over, light of one description was beginning to dawn, and that was the difference about the girls with whom I worked.

I remembered the comment made at my interview when I discovered, with anguish, that not only was Ruth deludedly religious but so were all the other four girls. They all belonged to some church or other and seemed to talk about little else.

Once a week they'd go off to a lunch-hour service in the city. They invited me, but I abruptly declined and went to Petticoat Lane market instead. I couldn't understand it and felt resentment that once again I was the odd one out, the different one again. My confidence was undermined and I seethed inwardly. Then one lunch-hour I let rip.

'Look here, I was brought up as a Jehovah's Witness, and lots of things you are taught to believe just aren't true. All this church business is no good. The Bible says God doesn't dwell in temples made with hands. And Jehovah God is going to smash all organised religion. What about the battle of Armageddon, the hundred and forty-four thousand, and the Trinity? How does that make sense? If God died on a cross then heaven was left empty and Satan could have taken full control. It's not reasonable.'

Out it all poured. I felt better for the release.

Ruth and the other girls who had been on the receiving end of my outburst listened calmly and smiled sweetly. That made me more furious.

I wanted them to argue back, to get annoyed, but there was no biting repartee, no sense of shock. Instead they started asking me questions about my present state, which I found most disconcerting: did I still belong to the Jehovah's Witnesses? if I didn't attend the meetings where did I go? why had I left?

I didn't find it easy to explain my present position in view of the torrent I'd just poured out. But one thing I made quite clear to them. I was not interested in going to any kind of church whatsoever, and I was thoroughly enjoying life.

Having made my mark, and to my mind declared a state of war against all the girls, I knew again something of that stirring feeling of being persecuted for righteousness sake. Of course, there was no persecution, but it helped my trained, conditioned mind to accept the situation far more easily by believing I was something of a martyr and therefore gloriously different from these churchgoing, hidebound, deluded souls.

The obvious enthusiasm of those office girls for church involvement left me cold. If they had shown an aggressive or argumentative attitude towards me, I still wouldn't have been impressed.

What was effective, though I'd never have admitted it to them, was their attitude of love and concern for me as a person, never mind my background or belief. I could not fight against that. In my rebellious and confused state, covered with an icing of self-sufficiency and pleasure, I concluded they were a dreary and dull lot.

Some years later I learned that those girls prayed for me. Had I known at the time, I should have scorned them. I didn't need anything like that. I revelled in going my way.

After eighteen months, I left the office where the girls were 'different' to begin my long-desired career in journalism. It was a time of great elation and egotism. I was so glad to be free of those stuffy girls and to make a fresh start.

Especially now that I had met Alan who was three years older than me with a sophisticated man-of-the-world air. He was living in the fast lane and, in joining forces, life became doubly exciting, a breathless cavalcade of all-night parties, pubs and pleasure, fashion and frivolity. I felt I was standing tiptoe on the brink of a wonderful future.

There was nothing more I wanted.

10

SOMETHING IS MISSING

Just a few months had passed in my world of journalism. The feeling of elation and the glamour of the job had dimmed a little, but life with Alan was still wonderful.

Then, one lunch hour, walking down Victoria Street, I began to feel strangely disturbed, unsettled. I couldn't think what was the matter with me. It was a kind of dissatisfaction, a feeling of a vacuum inside me, a hollow needing to be filled or a loneliness perhaps.

I dismissed it initially, thinking it would pass, but from that time on it kept on coming. I was not conscious of it every single day, but the times this strange feeling did descend upon me became more frequent and more disturbing.

Whatever was the cause?

It was inexplicable and I mentioned it to no-one. Everything outwardly remained the same. Life was full of activity, I'd fallen in love with Alan, that was new, but surely that wouldn't produce such a feeling of discontent and emptiness.

The connection between this feeling and anything to do with God or religion never occurred to me. Since leaving my Bible-reading colleagues I'd had more opportunity to bury deeper all of the past. The subject had not been provoked at all since those days of my first job. And I certainly wasn't going to divulge my religious past to Alan.

We never talked about anything serious, life was too busy and full of fun. Alan had told me he'd once been the leader of a youth club at a Methodist church and used to go to the church on a Sunday evening, 'only to meet the girls' he said with a knowing look. I hadn't enquired further.

There was just one occasion when things of the past came flooding back. We cycled to Southend one Bank Holiday and came across a Kingdom Hall in a back street. People were pouring out the door as we passed.

Briefly there was an unhappy feeling of being completely on the outside, lost and apart from everything I had once known. I said nothing to Alan, but found myself wondering if I could ever go back to that. The roots were deep in my childhood years and I felt nostalgic, but not for long.

About this time I began meeting Pauline in the lunch hour. She was someone I'd met through Alan, one of his youth club friends, and she worked near to me.

We would wander along to the cloisters of Westminster Abbey to sit and have a good heart-to-heart. We warmed to one another as we shared our ideas on all sorts of things and one day I tentatively broached the things that had been bothering me for some while.

I told Pauline about the feeling of emptiness and dissatisfaction that seemed to hover round me. Much to my surprise Pauline understood perfectly what I meant for she had experienced a similar thing.

It costs to share ourselves, to open up honestly to another person because of the fear of being hurt, but I felt I could open up a bit to Pauline as she seemed to understand.

It was she who brought the subject of faith and God back into my thinking. Although not a convinced Christian herself, nor a follower or member of any religious group, she still kept the connection with the Methodist Church and went along most Sundays. 'Makes me feel better somehow,' she said, 'but I'm still seeking.'

Up to this point I hadn't associated this strange feeling inside with anything to do with a belief in God, my rebellion against my background and anything labelled religious. I thought the lid was firmly shut on that corpse. I did not expect a resurrection.

But Pauline was sure it was all linked up somewhere. She'd had long talks with another friend who had made a great impression on her. This friend had told her that she found in her faith something so utterly satisfying there was never any emptiness. She also told Pauline that whereas once she had been shy and painfully reticent, her confidence had been made so strong, by what she had found, that she could now go anywhere without embarrassment or fear.

This really impressed me although it was beyond my understanding.

'I don't see,' said Pauline, 'how anyone can be absolutely sure they've found the right faith when there are so many different ones in the world.'

I did not see either, yet once I had been very sure indeed. What a hopeless mess it all seemed to be! It seemed impossible that there could be a way out. Then something happened for which I can offer no explanation but God.

I came down to breakfast in the usual rush to get off to work. There was a letter for me. I looked at the writing on the envelope and the postmark, neither of which were familiar and then I opened it.

A feeling of shock went through me as I glanced at the contents, for this was no ordinary letter. There was no address of sender, no signature, but written in a clear bold hand at the top of the page were the words: 'Jesus said: I am the Way, the Truth and the Life, no man cometh unto the Father but by me'.

The letter went on to outline different religions such as Buddhism and Confucianism and show briefly where they fell short. It ended up by stating that Christianity was the only true way and, at the bottom of the page in capital letters, I read: 'YOU HAVE TO GO TO CALVARY'.

It was as much as I could do to get out of the house before my mother noticed my trembling. I trembled because I sensed then that the missing link in my life was something to do with God, and not so much that I was searching for him - I wasn't - but he was seeking for me!

I felt pursued and I trembled, as anyone might, who had an image in their mind as I did, of a great and awful Jehovah God whose laws I had defied, whose service I had scorned, and whose Name I had counted as nothing.

Arriving at the office I made a quick phone call to Pauline, giving her a brief résumé of the letter. 'It ends up saying you have to go to cavalry, what's that mean?'

'The word is Calvary,' corrected Pauline. 'Don't you know that's the place where Christ was crucified?'

No, I didn't know.

'It frightens me, who could have sent it? Do you think someone has overheard our conversations in the Abbey? But then how would they know my address?'

Pauline was as mystified as I was, but not so bothered. The one thought that prevailed was that it was something to do with those girls I used to work with. I might mention here that a few years later I did revisit those girls to tell them I had become a Christian and I mentioned the anonymous letter. But they assured me they'd had nothing to do with it.

I never discovered the source, but God must have moved the heart and hand of someone to send it for it was another link in the chain of events leading to my conversion.

After this I felt more and more restless. Yet on the surface all was the same and I told no-one except Pauline of my feelings.

Soon after this episode I was looking through the bookcase at home for something to read on the train. My eyes lighted on a very old copy of *The Pilgrim's Progress* by John Bunyan.

It was inscribed to my mother, her Sunday School prize for good attendance, and I felt drawn to read it. This seemed quite out of context with my life and attitude at that time, but God who knows us so completely, was pressing the need deeper. I was fascinated as I read it and often a peculiar trembling came over me. I had no control over it and no explanation for it.

But all I knew at that time of restlessness and inner emptiness was that many of my friends were talking of engagement and marriage, and it wasn't long before Alan and I were doing the same. Marriage must be what I need, I thought, and certainly in the excitement of that forthcoming event, the strange restlessness subsided.

11

MARRIAGE IS WHAT I NEED

Some people may never go to a church until the day they get married. If I had had my way, I shouldn't have been inside one on that occasion either. Everything in my upbringing still rebelled against the thought of anything to do with church. 'I think it's hypocritical to get married in a church when you never go,' I explained to the tall, dark and handsome young man I'd fallen hopelessly in love with.

Secretly, I felt sure my father would never consent to come to a church wedding. But rather than face up to this fact, which I could only imagine would be somewhat painful, I opted for the explanation about feeling a hypocrite.

Alan shrugged indifferently, a little surprised at such high moral thoughts. But he had been to church regularly, of a Sunday evening, before he joined the tennis club and met me. His motives had not been entirely pure in this, as he freely admitted.

As a leader at the church youth club he had a few friends, mostly blue-eyed blondes or vivacious brunettes of course, and church on Sunday evenings provided another meeting-place for fellows and girls with nowhere else to go.

He would be happy to get married at his Methodist Church, but if I thought a Registry Office - well what did it matter anyway?

I had not said much to Alan about my upbringing, or my conversations with Pauline and the sense of searching for something in life. He would, I felt, dismiss such things as of no real interest and it would spoil our relationship. We both, on the surface, held life lightly with lots of laughter. Anyway, at nineteen I thought that marriage was what I needed, and I looked forward to getting away from home and putting the past even further behind me.

Once, when Alan was at our house, Dad started steering the conversation to the Bible and world events. I groaned inwardly, feeling tension because of the treatise that was coming.

Dad was still an intense Bible student, but without the assistance of the Watchtower books. He met regularly with others, who had also left the organisation and shared with them his findings. And although he no longer went on the doors, he was never reluctant to witness to anyone who crossed his path.

'You see, Alan, I've studied the Bible for over thirty years and I know what it says about the things that are happening in the world ...'.

I cringed as conversation turned quickly into pontification, and Alan sat listening with grim expression and growing impatience.

When he was finally able to get a word in, it came out fiercely, like a tiger springing on his prey. 'Well, I'm an atheist myself and I think the Bible is a lot of mumbo jumbo. I'm more interested in Communism.'

I stood up quickly to indicate it was time to leave and to avoid further confrontation. But standing on the doorstep, saying goodnight, I started to cry.

'You're not really a Communist, are you?'

'What's that got to do with anything. What does it matter?' he growled.

I drew back from him fearfully. 'And don't you believe in God at all?'

'I don't know really, but I can't take all that stuff about the Bible.'

I could sympathise there, it was my father's dogmatic tone that made it so hard to hear what he was saying. We parted frigidly that evening.

Miserably I tossed and turned in bed, wishing I had not had such a different upbringing, and that my family were just ordinary, like everybody else, and that I'd never so much as heard of Jehovah's Witnesses. The whole association with that organisation had become my skeleton in the cupboard.

And with someone like Alan and marriage on the scene, I could see the spectre emerging to spoil everything. Any more evenings like this and he'll just think I'm some kind of freak, I thought.

But it didn't happen again. I made sure of it by

never letting my Dad and Alan be together for any length of time. And as for us, and our doorstep disagreement, nothing more was said. We just concentrated on enjoying ourselves as usual.

The date and time were fixed. And the place was to be the Methodist Church. I could hardly believe my ears when the suggestion came from Dad that we should get married there!

'I've been thinking,' he said. 'Alan knows the people there and we want somewhere to invite guests to ... and it will be just a simple building, more like a hall, no pomp or show. I don't mind going there ...' he rambled on.

I stared at him, eyes oozing with incredulity and my brain frantically thinking how I was now going to explain everything to Alan who had been completely convinced by my reasons for not having a church wedding.

Somehow it all worked out and I think we all ended up in church for different reasons. My Dad was taken up with the idea of having an important part to play in the ceremony. I welcomed the picture of the traditional bride, with all the trimmings. Alan got a bit nostalgic about his past connections with the church youth club. My in-laws were shocked at the idea of a registry office wedding - 'Not quite proper,' said Alan's Mum. And my mother was placidly acquiescent as usual and in her finest role as peacemaker.

So there we were, on that April morning in 1952, spending one of the most momentous occasions of one's life in an atmosphere that, to me, was quite foreign. But the surroundings were simple and peaceful and the minister was kind and friendly. He didn't drone or chant, he talked like a human being. I was amazed. There was a plain wooden cross on the wall, but I averted my eyes from that.

We sang 'The Lord's my Shepherd, I'll not want' and I enjoyed it, especially the bit about 'and my cup overflows', because that's how I felt. Life and love were overflowing. Could there be any happier moment?

From the glamour of the wedding we went straight to 'Laughing Water' - our name for the two-up, two-down terraced house in the road I had always lived in. We had bought it from 'Oakie', an elderly ex-Jehovah's Witness who wanted us to have it, complete with contents.

'Don't worry about moving anything, we'll sort it out,' we blithely assured her.

'Thank you, dears,' she said gratefully and departed to live with a relative.

It was just as well we were at the stage of 'love's young dream'. The dark brown paintwork, faded velvet-covered chairs with sagging hessian and bulging stuffing, cupboards crammed with chipped crocks, tins of dried milk, paper bags, corks and curiosities had failed to deter us from moving in straightaway. The one brass tap at the kitchen sink, the outside lavatory, false teeth in a cup and stale fat in a saucepan - what did that matter? It was all good for a laugh, especially when friends dropped in.

And drop in they did from the start, mainly thanks to Alan's breezy and liberal invites to do just that. At first it was disconcerting to me who had never experienced this style of hospitality. Jehovah's Witnesses visitors - and there was rarely any other sort - to my home, only came by appointment. The best china, the kept-wrapped-in-tissue tablecloth, the extra special food, had all to be ready for our guests. Now, in my own home, things were to be very different.

'Shall we go to church next Sunday evening?'

I could hardly believe it was Alan speaking. But he wanted to see some of his old friends - of course! No doubt that would result in a further influx of droppers-in. Not until we were seated in the Methodist Church, scene of our wedding vows, did I discover it was to be a Youth Service.

Immediately I felt apprehensive. My Jehovah's Witness indoctrination had been very strong on the evils of youth groups in churches. And I had never forgotten the guilty feeling that had gripped me when Vera had persuaded me to pop into the church youth club one evening.

Words from the past floated back: 'These youth clubs are an insidious attempt by the religionists to ensnare young people in their net of false teaching and religious humbug. Keep away from them'. I was no longer under my father's authority. He was no longer in the Jehovah's Witnesses. But the words remained and I could not relax.

Supposing they marched down the aisle carrying the flag? Vera had told me the Brownies did this in church sometimes. And that was idolatry, a heinous crime that I did not wish to witness.

But the service was beginning. No sign of the Union Jack. With relief I sat back and began to listen with interest to the three people, not much older than me, who spoke in turn after the singing of a hymn.

My mind wandered at first, trying to connect this new experience with something in the past, as we are prone to do for our security's sake. Yes, there was something similar at the Kingdom Hall sometimes when students in the Theocratic School 'practised' their speaking ability on the congregation.

I came back with a jolt hearing someone saying enthusiastically: 'And then Christ stood before me and I received him and my whole life was changed.'

I looked at the speaker. Her words paralysed any further reminiscences. What was she talking about - 'Christ stood before me'? I'd never in my whole life ever heard anyone say such a thing, although I'd heard plenty of things about Christ Jesus, the Logos, who had paid the ransom sacrifice, who'd invisibly returned in 1914 to set up the kingdom.

But seeing Christ standing in front of you - how could you? What did she mean? I wanted to ask Alan if he knew. I glanced sideways, his face was impassive and I thought I'd better wait.

After the service when we stood chatting with others, I kept looking at the girl whose words had so disturbed me. She seemed quite normal, laughing and talking with others.

'Who is that?' I asked Alan.

'Hilda Jay, she's going to be a missionary or something like that.'

'Did you understand what she was talking about just now?'

He shrugged and gave me a sort of vague look that meant he really hadn't a clue.

I wanted to go and talk to Hilda, but I felt afraid. Was she deluded by some emotional belief? It certainly sounded like it to my Watchtower trained mind. We concentrated on knowledge of the Bible, of knowing about Jehovah God and his purposes. Emotional experiences didn't come into it.

We never went again to the church, but some months later two people came into our lives, saying the same as did Hilda. And a whole lot more besides!

Peter and Betty were people like us, young and just married. Yet they were not like us we soon discovered. They were different.

Betty was a schoolfriend who got back in touch and suggested a get-together with our newly-acquired husbands. We arranged a Saturday evening meal at our house.

'What are they like?' said Alan.

'I don't know about Peter, but Betty was always very lively, often in trouble for giggling in class. I used to sit behind her and ...'.

Alan cut in with a groan, commenting pointedly, 'I shall look forward to meeting Peter.'

But within ten minutes of their arrival, his expectations of a man-to-man chat were somewhat shattered.

'What's the badge, Peter?' Alan leaned conversationally across the meal table.

In reply, Peter grinned and removed the shield-shape lapel badge and handed it over for inspection.

I glanced at it casually, and suddenly my whole body stiffened. I could sense Alan's tension too. On the badge the words were clear: 'Ambassador for Christ'.

'Nice,' muttered the man in my life, nonplussed for words for once.

I didn't trust myself to say anything. My thoughts were exploding like fireworks. What did it mean? What did he wear that for? Was it a club or something? Alarmingly, I felt the edges of my self-centred life were being once again infiltrated by something that smacked of that deadly thing called religion.

'What church do you go to?' Alan was quickly compensating for his stupid 'nice' remark.

‘A Pentecostal church,’ Peter’s grin spread into a broad smile as he spoke, and his eyes were twinkling.

I glared at Betty. She’d never been religious at school. Why had she married this strange man? Abruptly I changed the subject.

For the rest of the evening I was anxious to steer the conversation away from badges, churches, or anything remotely connected. It was a good evening with lots of laughs and I began to feel that these new-found friends were quite normal after all. They insisted on helping to wash-up before leaving and also insisted on fixing a date for us to visit them, for a meal.

‘I’m going to look it up,’ said Alan, hiking the dictionary out of the bookcase.

‘Good idea,’ I yawned indifferently, ‘I’m going to bed.’

‘Listen, it says here seven weeks after Easter.’

‘What on earth are you talking about?’

‘Pentecost, a Jewish festival held on the fiftieth day after the Passover; the festival of Whitsuntide, seven weeks after Easter.’

He looked up with a blank stare. ‘That was what Peter said, wasn’t it?’

I shrugged, ‘Think so, so what! Sounds peculiar to me. How can you go to a seven weeks after Easter church? Another stupid and deluded lot of religious people I suppose.’

‘They didn’t strike me as stupid or deluded.’

‘No!’ I sighed, ‘there is something different about them.’

‘Well, I’m going to ask Peter about this Pentecost thing next time.’

12

A DISTURBING ENCOUNTER

Peter slowly drew a thin black book out of his pocket as Alan pursued the meaning of 'Pentecostal' with him.

I had been chatting to Betty, but my attention was now riveted on that little black volume in Peter's hands. There was no mistaking what it was. But church people who carry a Bible around in their pocket! That was a new one to me. And it was mind-blowing that this was happening in our front room!

Peter opened the book and began reading:

> 'When the day of Pentecost had come, they were all together in one place. And suddenly a sound came from heaven like the rush of a mighty wind, and it filled all the house where they were sitting. And there appeared to them tongues as of fire, distributed and resting on each one of them. And they were all filled with the Holy Spirit and began to speak in other tongues, as the Spirit gave them utterance.'

Looking back to that moment now, I believe it was perhaps the best starting place for a Bible discussion for anyone with Jehovah's Witness teachings in their head. The Holy Spirit is not a subject that the Witnesses pay much attention to. So straightaway it gets away from the 'party line', from the set paths of approach and memorised Bible references.

Peter launched from his Bible reading into explaining how the events in the early church were being experienced now.

I felt paralysed with sheer unbelief at what he was saying. How could someone who was not a Jehovah's Witness possibly expound the Bible? I thought church people never read their Bibles, but just followed the traditions of men and listened to the vicar's sermons. And he never read his Bible either. He preached his own opinions.

Seeing Peter sitting in our front room, confidently turning the pages of Scripture and explaining to us what it said about the Holy Spirit, the combination of those two things made my head reel and my heart thump. Speaking in tongues, healing, gift of prophecy, interpretation ... I'd never heard anything about all this. Frantically my mind tried to connect these new ideas with the old.

Then I had it! Yes, of course, Peter and Betty must be spiritualists. Impatiently I butted in, glancing at Alan for support. 'Sounds like spiritualism to me.'

'What makes you think that?' Betty sounded surprised.

'Well, the Bible warns against contacting spirits and mediums. That's of the devil.'

'Is that what the Jehovah's Witnesses taught you?'

Peter's question made me jump. What did he know about my buried past? Betty, must have told him. She must have remembered from schooldays. I should have realised.

'Well, it's right, isn't it?'

'Certainly is!' They both nodded. 'But we're talking here about God's Holy Spirit, the third person of the Trinity, you know.'

'Know? I know there's no such thing as the Trinity. That's another weird idea church people have.'

I almost spat the words at him. Peter irritated me with his composure, his confidence in his beliefs, and I didn't want all my past churned up just now. Life with Alan was fun, we didn't need religion. And who did Betty's husband think he was, that he could tell me, a born and bred Jehovah's Witness, anything about the Bible?

As I became worked up, I sensed Alan becoming fed up. His questions about the word 'Pentecostal' were just academic. He wasn't wanting a full-scale Bible treatise.

'Let's have a cup of tea.' It was Betty coming brightly to the rescue.

'Good idea,' Alan responded quickly, but his clipped tone indicated 'end of conversation'.

The subject was changed. Peter slipped his Bible back into his pocket, and we got back to being friends, making silly jokes, and talking light-heartedly about this and that.

Once again on leaving, Peter and Betty insisted on fixing a date to meet again. I felt reluctant, but true to character, Alan breezily invited them along to our house for a meal the following week.

But the pattern of our evenings together, whether at their flat or our house, was set. Throughout that winter we met with Peter and Betty weekly, and however our conversation started it always led to some Bible discussion before long.

Much of the time it was Alan who led us into it with some provocative question: 'How can anyone believe God created the world in seven days? Where did Cain get his wife from?' I wanted to talk about things like Christ coming in 1914, Armageddon, and inheriting the earth, and the Trinity.

Peter would try to lead me from these mind-set tracks and get me floundering with uncertainty about 'being saved' as he would term it, the Holy Spirit, Jesus' death and resurrection. They knew that:

> What think ye of Christ? is the test
> To try both your state and your scheme.
> You cannot be right in the rest,
> Unless you think rightly of him.

I felt happy that Alan wanted to ask questions about the Bible because, although I did not want anything religious in our lives, a deep respect for the Bible was ingrained in me. (I can thank the Witnesses for that.)

And secretly I hoped these discussions would dispel any Communistic leanings he might still have. I had not forgotten our doorstep row, before we married, over his politics.

Slowly, my irritation with Peter changed into respect as his knowledge of the Bible continued to amaze me.

Of course, I had no idea what was going on behind the scenes that winter of discussion. Later I discovered that our friends quite deliberately avoided much mention of church, due to my inbred antagonism about such establishments.

But we never met with them on a Sunday. There was the unspoken understanding that they went to church that day. Thursday evenings were also out because, they explained, they went to church again.

Little was said about what they actually did on these occasions, and I for one wasn't going to enquire, yet. But Peter and Betty had told the people at the church about us, and had mustered a small group who prayed daily for us.

Wisely, our friends concentrated on seeing us in our home, or theirs, and looking into the Bible. They could not have laid the ground more effectively to bring us both into new life in Jesus.

Christmas came and went, but not without a great deal of regurgitated opinions from me on the fallacy of Christmas Day being the actual time of Christ's birth. And the hypocrisy of churches in using pagan symbols in their celebrations such as the tree and mistletoe.

Peter and Betty listened politely, not a feather ruffled by my words of condemnation. 'You're quite right,' Peter said with a grin. 'It's not the right date. But then Jehovah's Witnesses don't celebrate the birth of Christ on any date at all, do they?'

'No,' I replied feeling flattened by his agreement with me.

'And as for the pagan symbols, they're not objects of worship. There are no mystical properties or superstitions connected with them for Christians, of course.'

I shrugged indifferently, for my arguments were purely a practice of habit, a chance to display knowledge. I would be celebrating this first Christmas of our marriage with all the trimmings I could muster. There would be nothing religious about it, but we would be having a thoroughly good time with parties, theatres, late nights and lazy days away from work.

It was six months of weekly visits and endless discussion before they popped the question.

'How about coming to church with us this Sunday?'

Peter's casual tone was disarming. I felt no bristles rise, no simmering anger, but instead a strange inner longing to do just that.

I looked at Alan for his reply. I was not going to admit how I felt and hoped my face showed an impassive indifference as to what his answer would be.

'Yep, alright we will, OK?' He looked straight at me somewhat quizzically. I nodded, and the deed was done.

After they left, I sat wondering why I felt so willing to go. I had been so adamant against going, ever since that first evening we met Betty and Peter. And Alan! he seemed so affable about it all.

No doubt there were several factors that contributed to put us in this agreeable state. But the only one I was aware of at the time was that our curiosity had been greatly aroused by our discussions on the beginnings of Christianity and the reality of the Holy Spirit as recorded in the Book of Acts.

To me, who knew quite a few 'chapter and verse' quotes, and to Alan who knew none, there was something coming out from the Acts that drew us, despite our natural inclinations to avoid anything religious. And when our friends told us that the things we read of in Acts were happening then in their church, we were intrigued, amazed, fearful and unbelieving - they must be exaggerating of course.

The only way was to go and see for ourselves, which is what Peter and Betty invited us to do.

13

SOUND OF A CRY

Sitting on top of a number 54 bus one Sunday evening in March, en route for South Lee near Lewisham, I felt apprehensive. It was not just because of the unknown that was ahead, but I sensed a strange sort of longing within. I would not admit this to anyone, and the best way of concealing my feelings from the present company was to talk, loudly and quickly, about anything external.

'Why do you travel such a long way to church?' This was a genuine puzzle to me. 'What's so special about this place at Lee?'

'Well, there aren't any Pentecostal churches nearer to us, and we feel we've found our spiritual home with this assembly.'

I nodded politely not understanding what Betty was saying. Her use of the word 'assembly' bothered me almost as much as the word 'Pentecostal'. But that at least was now a familiar word. 'Assembly' sounded peculiar applied to a church, my idea of church that is.

But then everything was peculiar at the moment, even Alan, who refrained from saying anything and just sat there on the bus humming quietly to himself.

I knew that humming habit was a sign that he too was feeling uneasy.

It wouldn't have surprised me if he'd suddenly thought of a very good reason why we couldn't continue the bus journey. But he didn't, he just left it to me to carry on with the scintillating conversation that I'd started.

'The building doesn't look like a church at all,' Betty was saying. 'It looks like a barn, or a large shed. It's nothing to look at.'

I smiled wanly and wondered why on earth a building like a barn or a shed should be called a church. A church had a steeple, a tower, stained glass windows, it looked forbidding. How could a barn-like building be a church? It didn't make sense.

But I wasn't going to ask any questions. I'd got enough to cope with for this particular evening and you usually got more than you bargained for when you queried things with Betty and Peter.

'Here we are,' said Peter cheerfully.

We had walked from the bus stop along a road of very ordinary-looking terraced houses and come to a halt by a large board with the bold inscription: 'Emmanuel Pentecostal Church'.

What did Emmanuel mean? Don't ask, don't ask! I cautioned myself. I gazed in disbelief at the building in front of us. It was just like a barn.

Grinning broadly, our friends steered us round to the back entrance of the barn, through a small kitchen room and then suddenly we stepped into the building. It seemed full of light, full of warmth and yes, packed full with people, some standing, some sitting, singing some rousing sort of song. Some waved their hands in the air and swayed as they sang, and everyone beamed smiles at us as we made our way down the aisle to the very front row.

'There's no room anywhere else,' apologised Peter. How were we to know he'd reserved the front row for us! And that everyone in the church had been told we were coming. This couple they'd been praying for were there with them tonight.

'Hallelujah!, Praise the Lord!' I felt vulnerable and nervous. The atmosphere overwhelmed me. Nothing had prepared me for this and if Peter and Betty called this place a church, I just could not. This was a plain hall of a building which seemed to vibrate with an unexplainable power.

When the minister and elders were assembled on the dais in front of us, a hymn was announced and the congregation rose to sing. I stood up, legs wobbling, and no sound would come from my lips. Feeling tense with fear, I wished I had not come.

But there was love, and warmth and joy, in this place that I could not deny. Something radical was going on inside me. I felt all the ground of criticism, hatred and mockery of anything to do with a church, that I'd stood on so long, was being swept away.

In my few previous visits to churches nothing like

this had happened. And this place was not like a church. The people were not the stereotypes that I'd clung to. There were chairs, ordinary chairs, not sombre hard pews. There was light in the place, not a gloominess. There were no crosses, just Bible texts.

On the front of the dais I read the words 'Jesus Christ - Saviour, Healer, Baptiser and Coming King'. Didn't God, Jehovah God, get a mention in this place? It was mind-blowing. So many barriers, built up for years, were being knocked down in one fell swoop.

A group of four young people came to the front to sing. I gazed up at their faces, hearing only the simple refrain 'It's in my heart, it's in my heart'. And I felt wistful for an unknown something I sensed in them.

A lady missionary was speaking that night. She just seemed to keep on about people out there in Africa who were 'coming to the Lord'. Whatever that meant, I could listen happily all the while we were 'in Africa', but then she homed in on her audience, particularly addressing her remarks to Alan and me in the front row. Well, that's how it seemed at the time.

I wriggled uncomfortably, but also felt indignant about her insistence that we needed to become Christians. She wasn't in Africa now talking to the heathen, was she? We lived in a Christian country didn't we? I felt confused.

Christian? Of course I was, because of all those years in the Jehovah's Witnesses, all that Bible knowledge tucked away, how could it be otherwise? I wasn't so sure about Alan, but he didn't seem too disturbed.

I glanced sideways at his rigid form, his face set like a flint. What was he thinking? I didn't reckon he was too thrilled about things at all.

It was so unbelievable that we were in this place on a Sunday evening anyway. I thought wryly of those Sunday evenings at the Kingdom Hall, the Watchtower studies, the people and the atmosphere there. But I could make no connections between then and now. This was something totally different!

The man leading the meeting was the pastor. Betty and Peter had told us a lot about Mr Barnes. He seemed very ordinary and I felt relieved that he wore a suit and tie and didn't look religious. It helped me to listen to what he said without having to vault over the 'obstacle' of a clerical collar. He was very insistent about anyone who wasn't a Christian coming to talk to him afterwards.

As we sang the last hymn he kept breaking in between the verses to repeat his invitation, to meet with him in the vestry. I wondered if anyone would. Anyway it certainly didn't apply to me. I started to button my coat, anxious to leave this disturbing place. But that wasn't going to be easy.

Just as we began moving towards the exit we were

surrounded by smiling faces, people wanting to be introduced, shaking our hands and chatting away as if we were long lost friends. 'The Lord bless you,' someone said. 'Lovely to meet you, so glad you have come.'

I was bewildered, especially as I got detached from Alan in the mêlée and panicked he might get out the door before me. Peter and Betty might not be in any hurry to leave, but I was. Eventually Alan grabbed me and hiked me through the throng.

The exit was in the middle of the building. Thankfully we didn't have to proceed all the way up that aisle again, through more people who no doubt would shake our hand and 'bless us' or whatever it was they were doing.

We reached the door, oh! horror, there stood the man, the pastor, shaking hands with everyone as they left. Did we have to? I only wanted to get out of this extraordinary place and get on an ordinary double-decker bus home. Only then would I feel safe and only then would my emotions calm down. We did the handshake, given with a penetrating look and 'God bless you' and moved out into the cool night air.

Whew! we made it!

Our friends joined us and we walked in awkward silence down the road.

Suddenly I stopped and clung to Alan sobbing.

'What's the matter?' he asked tersely.

'I don't know, I don't know.' I trembled as uncontrollable emotion swept over me.

'Don't be silly. Come on, let's go home.'

I felt alarmed as he pulled brusquely away from me. I didn't want to go home, not any more. Instead I felt a strange longing to return to the place we'd just left.

I stood there motionless as Alan walked on impatiently. He was angry, I knew, at my emotional exhibition. I wished it hadn't happened.

Peter intervened, gently suggesting we should go back and talk with the pastor, and Alan reluctantly gave in.

I saw the short, rotund figure of Pastor Barnes, still standing in the doorway as we approached. Why should we talk to this man? And once he found out my Jehovah's Witness past I doubted he would want to talk to me anyway. My inbred aversion to vicars and pastors, even without a collar, began to rise.

But here we were being ushered through the church to a small room behind the platform. Alan declined to sit down. He obviously didn't intend staying long.

When the pastor came in and sat beside me, Peter and Betty left. I would have preferred them to stay, feeling safer in their company. But I learned later they gathered with others to pray for us.

I sat wrapped in a shroud of unreality as Mr Barnes opened his big black Bible and began pointing out some verses to me. He asked me to read them aloud.

I tried through my tears. I heard words like 'sin', 'confess', and 'Jesus Christ', but I sat there bewildered and distressed. I hated the fact that Alan wasn't sitting beside me and felt vulnerable to my emotions.

'Will you pray and ask Jesus into your heart?'

I froze with fear. What was all this leading to? And why didn't he ask Alan? Why me? It was embarrassing, humiliating and quite, quite strange that I, a born and bred Jehovah's Witness, opposed still to every form of organized religion, despising the church and what it proclaimed, should be sitting, weeping, in a minister's vestry.

The fact that he pointed out scriptures to *me*, was a sickening experience. What would my parents think if they could see me? How could I go back on years of teaching and training and sincere belief, which it surely must mean if I were to accept anything that the pastor was saying?

Mr Barnes was waiting for my response. I had to say something. It was the only way this painful episode would be brought to an end, and I could escape. 'Dear God ... if there really is a God ... please come into my life and sort out the muddle?'

It was the sound of a cry, from a heart desperately longing for peace, a mind too befuddled to think clearly, and a person very fearful of just what all this meant. But I felt relief that I'd managed to say something.

Mr Barnes moved across to Alan standing firmly by the door, tall and stern with arms folded, and determined expression.

'And what about you, sir. What do you think?'

'I don't!' came the terse reply.

'Well, this is a very serious matter. I hope you will think about it.'

It was kindly spoken, but wisely nothing more was said.

'I think it's time we went home.' And with that Alan opened the door and with our friends started off down the road in silence once again.

There was little conversation as we travelled home. I for one was saying nothing. I'd said enough that evening and guessed Alan was simmering inwardly, livid no doubt about my naivety, stupidity and presumption in doing something without his agreement.

Peter asked us back for supper, and despite the strained relationship we felt, we went with them. I felt the evening had been a disaster. And it was obvious Alan had 'gone off' them, as well as me.

I would have given anything, at that point, for us never to have met Peter and Betty. It was all their fault we were in this present state of disturbance and unhappiness. If only it could all be blotted out, and we could get back to our normal life and leave all this religious business out of it forever.

Round the supper table we began talking about this and that, anything but what had just happened. I was just beginning to relax a bit when Peter handed me a small book saying simply, 'Now you're saved you ought to read this.' He spoke casually but his words hit me and I felt afraid.

Saved? How could I be? What did that mean anyway? I didn't like the expression, it sounded most strange, especially when applied to me. I wanted to shout at him, 'But I'm not saved. I shan't feel or be any different after tonight.'

I certainly didn't want to be different, mainly because I couldn't see our marriage lasting if I was. But I said nothing. I thought, 'Peter, you are quite wrong. This is an emotional upheaval which will pass.'

That night I lay awake a long time, mulling it all over. What had I done? I wasn't sure I'd really done anything except cry out my despair and confusion. And so what? Nothing had happened. Everything had come to an abrupt end and I'd just made a fool of myself.

I tossed and turned, cried into the pillow and felt thoroughly miserable. Alan hadn't spoken to me since we had come home. He was now fast asleep. I could only hope that, come the morning, it would all be forgotten and Alan would speak to me and life would be alright again.

But Monday came and went with little change. It was Tuesday morning when I woke early, after another restless, unhappy night, with a strong sense that something was different. I sat up, looking round the room at the familiar furnishings. Everything was just the same.

It was only as I washed and dressed that I realised the 'difference' was inside me. There was a calmness, a strange peace I'd never known before. Alan was there, still distant and uncommunicative, but I wasn't upset about it. There was a new something about me. It was a miracle, the miracle of new birth.

God had heard my cry and come into my life.

14

WE ARE DIFFERENT

One evening, a week later, we had become a little more communicative, and we set off to visit some friends who had just had their first baby. We knew them well and had spent enjoyable times together in the past.

But that evening I knew things were different because I was different. It was no longer possible to engage in pleasant chitchat. I had something to tell. I now wanted everybody to know and experience Jesus Christ living in their lives and making sense of life.

I waited for my opportunity, trying to manoeuvre the conversation round so I could 'get in'. Then they said something about the baby being christened and I took it as my cue.

'Why are you going to do that? What do you think it means, if anything? There's nothing real about it, unless you know Christ. You see, I've had this experience ...'.

The words tumbled out and when I finally stopped you could have cut the air with a knife. They stared at me and said nothing. I didn't care. I had told them the most important thing I knew. I had to do it. But what, of course, was so wrong was the outrageously rude manner in which I did it. Small wonder they were not impressed by my outburst. But I was only one week old and didn't know any better.

Not surprisingly, Alan was very annoyed and had a few sharp words to say as we journeyed home. 'If you're going to carry on like that, we soon won't have any friends left. I don't understand what you're saying anyway. And I'm sure they didn't. And if you think I'm going to become like you, you can forget it.'

He couldn't have flattened me more successfully. I realised miserably we just were not on the same wavelength and although I knew I jeopardised a friendship that evening, I longed that Alan might understand how I felt.

We had been married almost a year, I could sense that the gap which had come between us was only going to widen as time went by. How could our marriage work unless he found Christ too? The joy of my salvation was dimmed by the thought that the situation was impossible.

I had no idea then that the things which are impossible with man are possible with God. The God I was becoming acquainted with, through Christ, was not only a God of Love, but a God of miracles too - and One that answered prayer.

Prayer had never played an important part in my life, and I had never been taught anything about it. In the Jehovah's Witnesses the emphasis was always on service and study. But after that painful conversation with Alan, I felt desperate and found myself praying as never before. While engaged in my work each day I would be crying in my heart to God; I took every opportunity when alone to get down on my knees and plead with him for Alan, for us to be brought together in Christ.

Peter and Betty kept in constant touch with us, and we continued spending time at each other's home.

Alan eventually admitted that at least something had really happened to me and it was not just an emotional experience that looked like fading away. Something definite had taken place, a climax in my life and the process outworking from that was now beginning to show.

The desire that we should be together in what had happened was always uppermost in my mind. I had no theological arguments to present, no convincing discoveries of Bible truth. And at this stage, no clear idea just how what I had found differed from my Jehovah's Witness beliefs. I knew it was different because of what it had done to me inside. But there was to be a long sorting-out process, and many hurdles to be overcome, before I could say: 'I know *whom* I have believed, and am persuaded that he is able to keep that which I've committed unto him against that day' (2 Timothy 1:12).

Our Christian friends took us again to the church.

Alan agreed to come, I think only to prove to himself that he would not be affected by anything that was said. He could take it - and leave it. Of course, had he been aware that most people in the church were praying constantly that he too might be reconciled to God, he probably wouldn't have come along feeling so confident.

The lady missionary who had been on the platform speaking that night of our first visit, came over to talk to us.

'Are you happy in your new-found salvation?' she enquired sweetly.

"Only half-happy,' I replied, with tears welling up.

'It's all my fault,' Alan chipped in bluntly, 'I just don't understand what has happened and we don't see things the same way any more.'

'Could I come and visit you in your home one evening?'

'Certainly,' we said politely, hiding our surprise, shock even, at such an offer. I did not think it would do any good. Alan needed a man, like himself, to talk to him about such a delicate subject. He would surely be inwardly cynical of a woman's words. Women were so emotional.

Yet I know now that God answers prayer, often in the most unexpected ways. His accomplishments are not by might, nor by power, but by his Holy Spirit. Not by conventions, meetings, literature, witnessing in itself, but in the power of the Holy Spirit behind these things. He is the effective force. Jesus said: 'Without me you can do nothing' (John 15:5). How difficult it is to accept the fact that our own organized efforts and sacrificial service are not sufficient! The glory of any conversion, any marvellous work, is always due to the Lord and the power of his Spirit.

So it was in the most unemotional circumstances, and most unlikely situation, that Alan found Christ as his Saviour. Sitting round the fire in his own home, an aroma of fried onions, a gentle lady knitting and telling us of her life in Africa. But he said nothing that evening to indicate his inner struggle and I assumed he was unmoved by the visit.

I felt miserable but realised for the first time, the whole matter was completely out of my control. Which was the very best thing I could realise, if only I'd known it.

It was a few days before things began to focus for Alan and the inner feeling of being at peace with God and with himself began to outwork. It came when he confessed with his lips what had happened inwardly.

Our two friends came to the rescue in asking him point-blank if he was saved. Nothing like shock tactics, I thought, bracing myself for the retort which I thought must come. But he answered 'yes' and that was that. Of course I could hardly believe it. The thing I'd cried and yearned over almost day and night for the past six weeks had happened.

But when Alan came home from work next day and told me he'd been singing hymns as he cycled, and what's more, he'd discovered a colleague in the office who had been converted the previous day, there was no more breath in me. God had heard my cry and come into Alan's life.

So now for us both the outworking of a new life in Christ had begun. Alan did not have to disentangle his thinking from years of Jehovah's Witness indoctrination, as I did, and his progress was more rapid than mine. Yet today I often wonder if either of us would have advanced very far into the Christian life if we had not become involved, soon after our conversion, in service for God.

Faith is an act. To believe that Jesus Christ lives in us, by the power of the Holy Spirit; to know he has transformed utterly our ideas and way of life; to claim a constant sense of peace and real purpose in life, is a belief that cannot, must not, be kept to oneself. Everything God gives us, or shows us, is to be shared, in some way, with others. As the Bible puts it: 'He died for all, that those who live might no longer live for themselves but for him who for their sake died and was raised' (2 Corinthians 5:15).

We continued for some months to go to the warm and friendly church with our two friends. They were our earthly props, allowing us to lean on them while we learned to walk the pilgrim way. There was much to be discussed. Problems and difficulties of a new way of living, our lack of past church connection, made us feel like strangers in a strange land. We needed props.

There were several other young couples at the church who overwhelmed us with invitations to their homes for meals and friendship. We were amazed to find how normal they were, although different. We discovered it seemed a rare thing for a Christian to be without a sense of humour, and many were the hilarious and helpful evenings we spent with this one and that.

It was soon obvious that what they believed did not exist just on Sundays, and we found in them, as we had noticed with Peter and Betty, that their link with Christ influenced every single aspect of their life. And what he would have them do was always the first consideration. I thought often of the sincere and zealous workers and friends I had known in the Witnesses. There had been that same sense of influence over all they did. But it was the influence of an organization, a movement, rather than that of a Person.

Perhaps one of the richest earliest discoveries I made of life in Christ was the care he felt about individuals. There is no question of being pressed into a mould when Christ lives in you. He uses you as an individual.

I understood that sometimes certain individual traits had to be dealt with, or surrendered, in order to function fruitfully along with others in the church. But the God I was getting to know was not a dictator or slave-driver, he gently led me into and through these experiences. He did not seek for uniformity but unanimity.

Jehovah's Witnesses will boast 'We are one but Christendom is divided', a fact that appeals to many people who are confused by the various denominations they see around them. They have a uniformity of thought which is produced in each Witness by means of their literature, particularly the Watchtower magazine, studied together at the Kingdom Hall. But I was now en route to discovering a different oneness, a unanimity amongst Christians which is born and developed by the Holy Spirit working in us as individuals, relating in love to God and one another. This is the result of faith, not knowledge.

More and more, as weeks and months went by, I began to realise that the true Christian life is a life of faith. And my faith came to be centred more and more on Jesus Christ himself. I had joined no organization, I had not committed myself to any group or denomination, but I believed I now belonged to Jesus Christ and he would teach me the way to go.

It was still some while before I discovered that to follow him meant discipline in reading the Bible, praying, worshipping and witnessing. But God kept hold of Alan and I in those early stumbling days and led us into a work which was to be our training and school of experience in learning more about himself.

A Sunday School superintendent approached Peter and Betty and ourselves, asking if we would consider holding a regular Sunday evening service for the ex-scholars. The children met in a mission hall near where we lived, and there was no particular church connection. It was difficult therefore for them, as they grew up from the School to become incorporated into a church fellowship, and the superintendent had been very concerned about this for a long time.

The idea to us was very alarming, for we knew so little of the Christian life. Yet this was the way God chose to lead us on with himself. And although we made many mistakes, found ourselves beset by many problems, and not a few personal upheavals, we know it was all in the best of wisdom that this opportunity came to us. Acceptance of Christ as Saviour must lead into commitment and involvement in some way. There is really no room for passengers.

The Jehovah's Witnesses present a challenge to us in this regard because a person does not become a Witness until he is prepared to go out on the door-to-door work and give himself unstintedly to the proclaiming of the message. I have known house-proud women who abandoned their household duties in favour of working for God's kingdom, as well as young people, full of life, whose energies were harnessed to the one purpose of telling others Bible truths.

We imagine that we can call ourselves 'Christian' because we do God the favour of sitting in a pew on Sunday morning, or we have been a staunch member of some church group for many years. Yet we would not dream of leaving our home comforts on a winter's evening to go into someone else's home and share with them our discoveries of the Lord, and the Bible. And what is more, to assure them that their every need can be met in Jesus Christ.

Why won't we? Because, if we're honest in many cases we have no personal discoveries of the Lord to share. And we can assure no-one that Jesus is the answer to their needs because we have not proved him for ourselves. If only we would emphasise, particularly to the Jehovah's Witness who knocks on our door, that Christianity is a relationship, not a religion, it might well help to disperse the distorted views these people have of everything religious.

As we began the Sunday evening venture, I began to discover the joy of service in a way I'd never known, because it was not so much service *for* God (which is the Jehovah's Witness attitude) but service *unto* the Lord, which is a very different thing and can be carried out in every area of life.

We began to spend time visiting locally door-to-door as well as holding open air meetings round the streets, and we learned to share with others, in informal ways, the Good News about Jesus. The more we spoke, of course, the more we committed ourselves and, as Sunday followed Sunday, Alan and I knew we were becoming more and more involved. There could be no turning back and gradually we realised, with joy, we had no desire at all to go back to our old way of life.

But with the increasing sense of involvement, there came to me an increasing need for a great deal of rethinking and sorting-out of past ideas and beliefs from the present truth and light that was dawning. The new birth was a miracle, but it was only the beginning. By faith I had received the Lord Jesus Christ as my personal Saviour. But having received him, there now had to be a process of learning to walk in him, grow in him, and this, because of my Jehovah's Witness background, required some considerable thought reform.

15

RETHINKING ALL I EVER KNEW

'There's someone at the door,' shouted Alan from the front room where he was trying to burn off the dark brown paint.

As soon as I opened the door I knew why the person had knocked. But I stood silent while she introduced herself and her companion as 'Bible students calling in this area to bring you a message of hope in this troubled world'.

I let her talk on for a while as familiar words and phrases washed over me. I was playing for time, wondering how to explode into the parrot-like spiel with the message I knew I had to give her, when Alan joined me on the doorstep.

He didn't hesitate to break into the earnest words of the lady Witness, and clipping her sentence in mid-air, he told her how he had become a Christian. All he said was true, and I knew his heart was right, but his aggressive tone made me wince.

I had heard many Jehovah's Witnesses put their message across aggressively. But surely we should speak differently to them. I thought ruefully of some of the aggressive outbursts I had delivered in the name of witnessing, but I would be so much more careful with a Witness. I knew so well what fuel to their fires of hatred for anything religious this kind of encounter would be. The two ladies soon retreated from our door.

'Why didn't you say anything?' demanded Alan.

'I don't know, I was going to, but then you came ...'.

'I shouldn't have been so aggressive.'

'No. I was going to tell them how I became a Christian, but I didn't want to tell them I had been a JW and I knew everything that they were trying to tell us. Anyway I couldn't argue with them along their usual 'party' lines. I really am still confused about the difference between their beliefs and what I now think.'

Alan went back to his blowlamp without replying.

It was my particular problem, this rethinking. Everything we were learning came to him fresh. He didn't have the ingrained concepts and attitudes that I had. He had nothing to untangle. But I certainly did, and the question was where to start.

As it happened, I didn't sit down for hours of Bible study, but through being precipitated into the deep-end of involvement with young people coming to the Sunday evening gospel services we held, the unravelling began to take place on the job. It was also opportune that Billy Graham was in London at that time. For it was in listening nightly to his preaching that I realised the first thing to get clear was what did I believe about the person and work of the Lord Jesus Christ.

I had been taught, trained, to serve Jehovah God. I had great respect for the man Christ Jesus.

He was the first creation of Jehovah, the first of many spirit sons. Jehovah God was the Supreme Power and his son Jesus was subject to him always. He was the 'Word' prior to his coming to earth, the one who speaks and acts for Jehovah: 'In the beginning the Word was, and the Word was with God, and the Word was a god ...' (John 1:1 *New World Translation*). As chief of the angels and next to the Father, he was the Archangel Michael mentioned in the book of Daniel. Jesus laid aside his divine nature to become a man, with a perfect human nature, equivalent to Adam before the fall. He was not God incarnate.

If I still believed this I knew I could never accept the idea of God as a Trinity, and the co-equalness of the Father, Son and Holy Spirit. In the early days of my conversion this was confusing and I was unable to get clear in my thinking for a long time. I continued to feel uneasy about the very word 'Trinity', cutting as it did right across all my childhood teaching. And talking or arguing about it didn't seem to get me anywhere. It was a mystery, as the Bible says:

> 'For without controversy, great is the mystery of godliness: God was manifest in the flesh, justified in the Spirit, seen of angels, preached unto the Gentiles, believed on in the world, received up into glory' (1 Timothy 3:16).

So I left it at that. I accepted that there is much of mystery in 'the Trinity', and it is impossible to fully comprehend an infinite God with a finite mind.

Later another verse of scripture came vividly alive to me and brought a further dawning of light:

> 'For God, who commanded the light to shine out of darkness, hath shined in our hearts, to give the light of the knowledge of the glory of God in the face of Jesus Christ' (2 Corinthians 4:6).

Increasingly I realised that a personal knowledge of God was only possible to anybody through receiving Jesus Christ into their life. It was only in the person of Christ that I would find all of God that I was able to understand. Only Jesus made sense of God to me, for he dispelled the image of a far-off, vague, vengeance-seeking Being, and showed to me a God whose name was Love, who knew and cared about every individual person and who so loved me that he gave his only begotten Son that if I believed in him I should not perish but have everlasting life. Through the Gospels the Holy Spirit revealed Jesus to me as more than Saviour. He was my Friend, my Lord and my God.

Acceptance, or rather revelation, that Jesus Christ is God does not mean I believe in a God with three heads (which is what Jehovah's Witnesses think the Trinity must mean). But as we speak of a husband and wife being made one, yet they are two different persons, so it is conceivable that the Father, Son and

Holy Spirit are one, though three different persons. There is still mystery. But I live now by faith. If I could logically and rationally define God, then I am thinking of him only in human terms. The life of faith transcends knowledge.

It was a moving experience for me to partake for the first time in a Communion Service with other Christians. I felt over-awed that I should be allowed to do so, for I had attended the yearly Memorial Service held in the Kingdom Hall, only as an observer.

The bread and wine is only taken by those who know themselves to be one of the 144,000. This Memorial is celebrated by Jehovah's Witnesses on the anniversary of 14th Nisan in the Jewish calendar, which may fall on any day of the week, not necessarily Good Friday. It is, as I understood, held as a reminder of Christ's death, of his sacrifice, of the ransom whereby we may be saved to eternal life. This is seen as an important reason why Jesus came to earth. This Watchtower book also states:

> 'Explaining why he had come to earth, Jesus told the Roman governor Pontius Pilate: "For this I have been born, and for this (purpose) I have come into the world, that I should bear witness to the truth" (John 18:37, *New World Translation of the Bible*) .... Also, he said: "I must declare the good news of the kingdom of God, because for this I was sent forth" (Luke 4:43).[1]

---

1. *You Can Live Forever in Paradise on Earth*, page 60, pub. 1982.

And an issue of the Watchtower magazine states:

> '(the good news) includes the knowledge that Jesus offered a ransom sacrifice in our behalf. Without that sacrifice, our relationship with God, our very salvation - not to mention the kingdom of Jesus and 144,000 priests and kings taken from the earth would not be possible.'[2]

A Jehovah's Witness is taught that Christ died on the cross to atone only for Adam's sin. There is no personal application to the sin in one's own life; and the meaning of the cross in daily life, the cleansing from guilt and power of sin giving a victorious life, is a teaching I had never heard within the confines of the Jehovah's Witness organisation. It was some way along the path of my new life in Christ before these great facts were brought home to me, and made real in my experience by the Holy Spirit.

I was enjoying the Christian life. Alan and I were engaged in lots of activity and were being continuously surprised at the changes being wrought in us by the power of Christ. We had had a great experience, we had a great message to tell, yet we had to make the painful discovery that in all of this, wonderful as it was, there was a great core of *self* in both of us.

As the Lord led us gently on with himself, it was to this ugly core that he began to draw our attention

---

2. The *Watchtower*, 15 August 1991, page 17

- the discovery that *self* has to be crucified, the outworking of which is an on-going process. We learned much from Christian literature such as Watchman Nee's *The Normal Christian Life* and Roy Hession's *Calvary Road*. But suffice it to say that this tremendous aspect of true Christian living is virtually untouched by Witness teaching.

The greatest help to me in rethinking all I ever knew, was the realisation that the Christians, with whom we now kept company, based their faith on the Bible as the inspired Word of God. I had no problems in carrying over with me into my new life, the yardstick of God's Word by which to measure my life. I was, and still am today, deeply grateful for the heritage which had taught me to respect and value the Bible as 'the most precious thing this world affords'.

But I soon discovered that these Bible-believing Christians had more than just a head knowledge of the Bible. They knew God speaking to them through the words they read. Our missionary friend referred to the Bible as a talking book, and I was fascinated. The idea that God spoke to people personally was indeed something that Peter and Betty had intimated to us. Now as I met more and more people saying the same thing, I was presented with an exciting new way of reading the Bible. It was not that Bible study was no longer important or necessary, but rather that a whole new dimension was now open to me.

As I came to read biographies of Christians, especially of missionaries, this whole idea of communication with God through the Bible created a longing to experience this for myself. That meant spending time alone with God. As with any human relationship, there is no growth without spending time with one another, listening and talking honestly.

The opportunity I found for this, in a busy life, was when my three children were growing up. When Wendy was born in 1956 I gave up my job. Sharon arrived three years later, and in 1965 our family was completed with the birth of Lorna. Having to stay at home often, while Alan continued the active and involved lifestyle we had first shared, I grew resentful of the new restrictions on my life.

'I'm sure you realise your resentful attitudes have to go to the cross,' counselled a wise friend gently.

It was a painful but timely reminder that death to self was the only way forward. Once I set my will to do just that, the lonely evenings were transformed as, once the children were in bed, I discovered the delight of being alone with God and with his Word. And it was during those years that God built into my life a deep reservoir of faith and knowledge of himself. Prayer became a privilege, and God filled me with his Holy Spirit.

Whenever a Jehovah's Witness knocked at our door, then I was ready to stop them in their tracks and enthuse about a relationship with God. I still do this, and the reactions are the same as they ever were - a startled look, a wariness of anything so emotional, and a firm effort to get me talking instead about one of their familiar lines of approach.

'Everybody who belongs to Christ belongs to everybody who belongs to Christ.' The words of E. Stanley Jones became my favourite quotation when trying to explain to a Jehovah's Witness, or anyone else, what the real meaning of 'church' was.

I had been knocked sideways that first Sunday evening at Emmanuel Pentecostal Church, Lee, that such a barn of a place was called a church. When we began going there regularly I soon lost sight of the kind of building it was and realised that 'church' was all to do with the people who went there. As in the Book of Acts, it was people, believers in the Lord Jesus as their Saviour, who constituted a 'church'.

All my preconceptions were swiftly swept away, and many prejudices demolished, particularly when I discovered at this 'church' there were no such things as jumble sales, raffles or bazaars. Everybody brought a Bible with them to the meetings, prayers were made spontaneously, and people would stand up and speak of what God had done for them that week.

Later on I came to understand the concept of the Church as the Body of Christ. And then the perplexing issue of so many different denominations was resolved for me. I well knew that all the different churches was a fact that Witnesses on the doorstep would refer to superciliously, pointing out the great universal one-ness of their organisation. Now I could tell them, the inside story. Another quote that helped me get this issue in perspective was from Isobel Kuhn's *By Searching* - 'On our principles we must be adamant, but on our preferences we must be silent where it disunites the Body of Christ'.

I was taught in the Witnesses that the second coming of Christ occurred invisibly in 1914, and automatically accepted the reasoning behind this date. It was arrived at by calculation of various prophecies in the Book of Daniel. It was all tied up to the very date. It made you marvel.

But after being born-again such ideas were soon rejected for I read in the Bible that Jesus will come again, in power and glory, and every eye will see him. And there will be a miracle removal from the earth of all who know him as Saviour and Lord. I find also the warning, that the time of the second coming is known only to God the Father. We are told to live in a constant state of preparation for this event, like those who wait, watching and ready. Jehovah's Witnesses are waiting and watching for the battle of Armageddon, when only they will be saved.

I stand forever thankful to God for bringing me to himself and into the great company from every nation, tribe, people and language, throughout the ages - the Church, the Bride of Christ - who also wait for his glorious return.

POSTSCRIPT

When we became Christians radical changes took place in our thinking and lifestyle. And these were soon apparent to our parents and friends who were on the receiving end of some of our 'witnessing'. We were far from tactful and blundered in, at every opportunity, to talk about being saved, and urging them to consider their state before God.

Alan was more open with his parents than I dared to be with mine. I had to wait until some of the confusions in my mind were cleared before I could confidently say anything to them about my conversion. 'More open' Alan would admit is putting it mildly, and it was not surprising they did not take kindly to his outbursts. Alan's father summed things up wryly by commenting, 'Well, Son, it's been stamps, cycling, youth clubs and girls, and now it's religion. Don't worry, you'll get over it.'

But when Alan organised a coach to take his parents and several of their neighbours to a Billy Graham meeting, surprisingly they came willingly. Some even confessed later their regrets at not going forward on that occasion. And Alan's Dad, presumably realising his son was not just going through another phase or fascination, eventually acknowledged, 'You've got something.'

There was a tense period when our presence was reckoned to be a disturbing influence and, in fact, Alan's brother's house was declared 'off limits'. Then a few years later, Peter, his brother, became a Christian and that just about finished it for their puzzled Mum and Dad! However, soon they began coming to church for special events, and there seemed to be a greater thoughtfulness, a seeking after God.

When his father had a heart attack on holiday and was in hospital, Alan sent him a card with the 'usual' scripture text! He read it and said to his wife, 'I shall be alright now.'

He died the following day and Alan's mother said quietly, 'I shall give my life to God now and live for him.' And she did.

There is no doubt my parents and grandparents were aware of changes in my life, although little was said. For one thing, living in the same road they could not fail to notice the gospel poster which Alan consistently displayed in the downstairs front window. I knew my parents continued to meet with other ex-Jehovah's Witnesses and my father was still a devout Bible student, particularly of Bible prophecy.

But they must have said something to my sister and brother-in-law because we received a 'summons' from them to go and explain what had happened to us. We went happily, anticipating they must want to get saved. We talked eagerly of how we had become Christians, but their response was disappointingly clinical. They wanted the facts, but saw no need of faith for themselves.

That evening proved to be the precursor of innumerable times in the years following; every time we met, in fact, there would be discussion, debate, heated exchange of views as we contended for the faith. They remain unconvinced today but would not deny that it has 'worked' for us; it has lasted, there has never been any turning back.

We kept open house and encouraged friends to 'drop in any time'; we anticipated talking to them, explaining the way of salvation. They dropped in alright, although some only came once and we lost touch with them.

Pauline, my lunchtime confidante in the cloisters, came only once. I was sure she would want what we had found, for she was a seeker. But no, the emphasis we made on a personal relationship with God was too much for her to take on board.

I remember explaining to Pauline how I had told God he had to do something with Alan or we just couldn't go on together. I thumped arrogantly on the table as I spoke.

Pauline looked at me with whimsical expression and commented crisply, 'I'm sure God must be very frightened of you.' Oh! ground open up! I'd got it all wrong and felt humiliated by her remark. Pauline would continue to go to the Methodist Church because she felt better for attending a service, but more than that she could not do. She had her own plans for her life and didn't wish to surrender the reins.

With Erica things were very different. I had not had much contact with her since leaving school. She had come to our wedding and was now a primary school teacher. I wanted so much to tell Erica about becoming a Christian although I doubted she would be very interested. Erica, so self-possessed, so poised, so capable of so many things. She wouldn't have any need.

I telephoned her and invited her over. She came, but I just couldn't get the right words out. I rambled on about meeting up with Betty from school, and her husband, and how they'd taken us to church, which wasn't like a church at all. Eventually Alan cut through my tangled threads of talk with some clear matter-of-fact statements about our becoming Christians. Erica's eyes widened with curiosity and soon we were arranging to take her along to Emmanuel Pentecostal Church the next Sunday.

It turned out to be another memorable evening in that barn of a place. The service was given over to highlighting missionary work and several of the congregation had dressed up to bring an authentic touch of the different countries represented. I felt so anxious that Erica would appreciate this.

But when the meeting started and a procession of tambourine-shaking, hallelujah shouting, colourfully robed people, from every tribe and nation, filed down the centre aisle, I forgot Erica. I tried so hard to suppress the laughter that surged up within me, and I could see Betty having the same problem. It was such an unexpected and strange spectacle, controlling the giggles took all my concentration. With a nudge from Alan, who was quite straight-faced about it all, I calmed down and remembered Erica sitting next to me. What on earth would my quiet, intelligent, sophisticated friend think of this performing troupe! I felt anguish that she should come to church on this evening of all evenings. She probably wanted to leave – straightaway. But Erica was sitting transfixed by the procession in the aisle, not a flicker of amusement or anxiety in her expression.

It must have been well over an hour later when I was startled by Erica tying to push past me into the aisle. We were singing the closing hymn, the pastor was appealing for those to come forward if they didn't know Jesus as their Saviour. Open-mouthed I watched Erica walk to the front. I couldn't believe my eyes.

Erica became a Christian that night and never looked back. She began teaching a children's group at the church, using her professional skills and beautiful, singing voice. She eventually married one of the deacons and has continued to live happily ever after.

Three years after our conversion we moved to a bigger house, some distance from my parents, where we could continue keeping an open home on a much larger scale. We kept in regular contact with them, but our relationship was never easy, for our new way of life was taking us along a very different route to theirs. When we visited, there would often be a clash with my father who was so anxious to impose on us his knowledge of the prophetic Scriptures, and his condemnation of the Trinity. And we came away many times perplexed at the great gulf there seemed between us, although he declared his faith in Jesus as his Saviour.

But my parents were never willing to meet together with other Christians, they met only with a group of ex-JW's, and the anti-church attitude remained. We were therefore very surprised and delighted when they came to church for our children's dedication and, later on, to Wendy's baptism at a Pentecostal church. They were genuinely pleased about these events for us.

They had little idea of the things that were going on in our house, and we felt it was probably better they didn't know! A Christian family lived with us at first. Then came the busy years of our own family. We had Saturday evening 'squashes' in our front room, often with a missionary speaker from WEC

(Worldwide Evangelisation Crusade); as well as a bookroom in our home which channelled books from Christian Literature Crusade into the community. In addition there were regular droppers-in and a variety of lodgers.[1]

Our involvement in the Sunday evening gospel services at Woolwich came to an abrupt end when the building burnt down! But many of the teenagers were already making their way to our house on Dartford Heath every Saturday.

Alan would go out preaching Sunday evenings but found his forte in running children's campaigns and presenting the gospel in Christian Union meetings in local schools.

Involvement in the lives of people who came to our home was quite intense and eventually put our marriage under strain. But God provided a caring house group, in our home, who helped us sort ourselves out. Once all the children were at school I trained to teach Religious Education in a large comprehensive school.

We have moved house again in recent years in response to a request to take a lead in a small Elim Church in the village of Meopham, near Gravesend. (Amusingly this building has been likened not to a barn, but a shed!). And we continue to 'grasp those things for which Christ has grasped us'.

---

1. The story of the use of our home is told in *There's Somebody At The Door* published by SPCK Triangle 1985).

I was motivated to start writing when we met Derek Sangster, the then editor of *Challenge* newspaper, at a houseparty in Devon. We had been invited there as a family, and Derek encouraged me to try writing a regular column on family life for the *Challenge*.

I joined the Fellowship of Christian Writers some years ago and through that became a member of the Christian Writers postal circulator (started by Mary Driver, Director of the Sean Dorman Manuscript Society). I was greatly helped with the manuscript of this book by the 'crits and comments' and encouragement of the circulator's members and I am grateful to Ann Edwards for allowing me to use her poem which was prompted by this book.

THE SOUND OF A CRY

The sound that I hear
is the sound of myself
coming to the place where
there shall be no retreat.

The cry that I hear
is the sound of myself
standing naked, in fear
before the grace of God.

The cry that I hear
is the sound of myself

not understanding here
is my soul's salvation.

The cry that I hear
is the sound of myself
coming slowly to near
where His love will heal me.

The cry that I hear
is the sound of myself
giving up my will, mere
child I am before God.

The cry that I hear
is the sound of myself
giving up tho' in tears,
my life, to God Himself.

The cry that I hear
is the sound of myself
    in my smallness
before the encompassing
    greatness of God.